easy
HOT & SPICY

THE AUSTRALIAN Women's Weekly

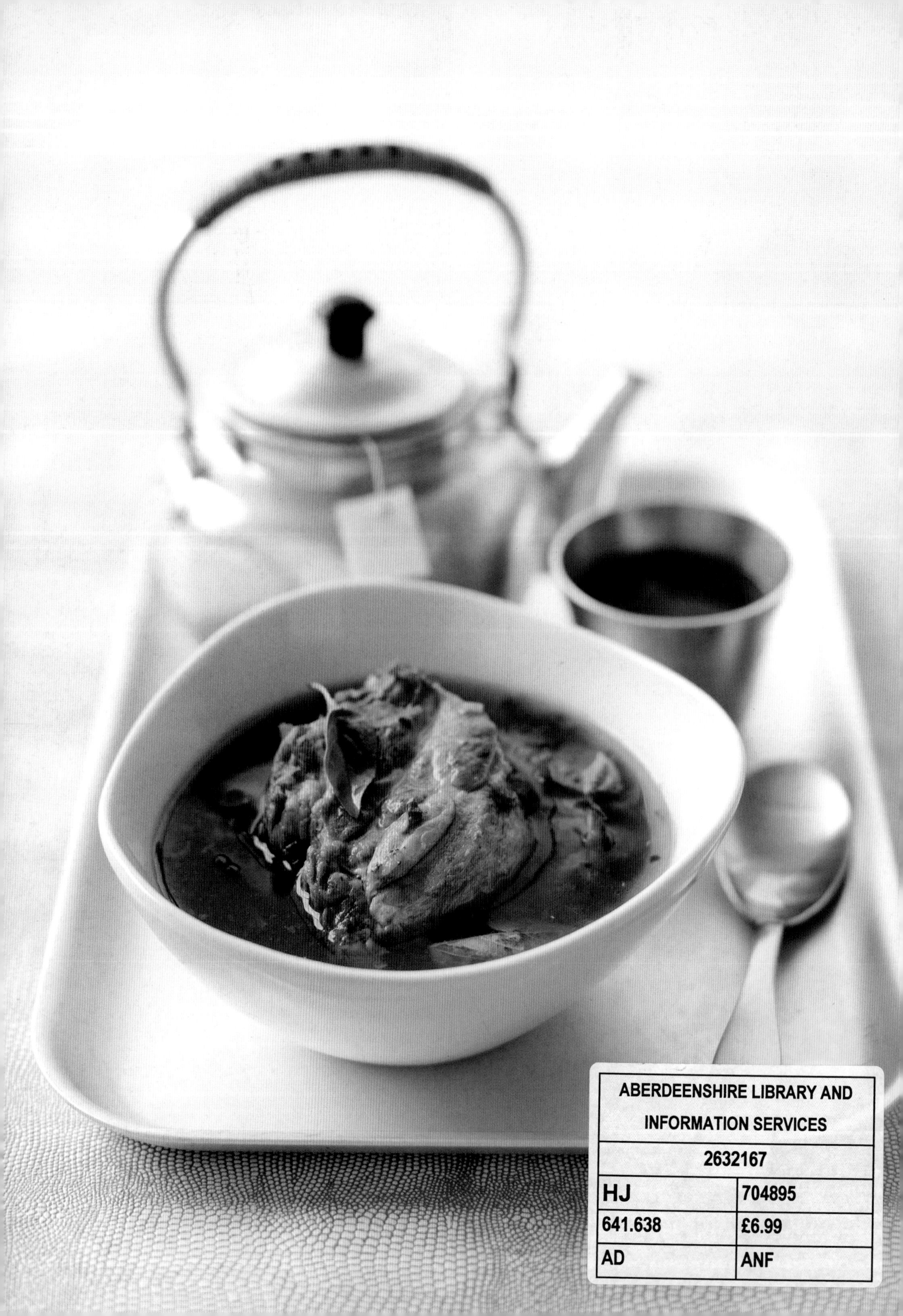

contents

We draw our food references from so many different countries these days, that sometimes it is almost impossible to say where a recipe originated. If you like your food richly warm with the depth of spices, you will find lots of new ideas to cook in this collection of recipes chosen just for the kick! Not just the obvious curries and chilli recipes, and not just the hottest either: try a wider look at the world's spicy food.

Food Director

Pamela Clark

the spice of life

The fragrant aroma of a curry wafting from the kitchen stove stimulates the appetite and evokes memories of meals savoured in many an Indian eatery over the years, as well as those enjoyed more recently in Malaysian, Thai and Vietnamese restaurants. As food lovers, we've embraced curries, no matter what their country of origin, as one of our favourite foods, and one we like to make at home: here you'll find a selection of those that may have been born anywhere from Burma to the Caribbean, but which have been adopted with love as our own. Generally accepted as originating from *kari*, a Tamil word for a spicy or seasonal gravy or sauce, a curry is basically just that; while the recipes vary from country to country, and even region to region, most share the common denominator of being wet and savoury. From an incendiary Goan vindaloo to a mellow Kenyan stew, from traditional robust lamb and chicken mixtures to lighter seafood and vegetable dishes new to our repertoires, there's a curry to suit all tastebuds and occasions. Whether you use prepared curry paste or make your own, it's most important that it be of a very high standard, an amalgam of herbs, aromatic spices, dried and fresh chillies and, on occasion, fruits, seafood, stems, roots or nuts, crushed or ground together to make a complex, intensely flavoured ingredient.

Accompanied by a fluffy rice dish or a homemade bread, a tasty relish or dipping sauce, and a platter of cooling fresh greens or a bowl of raita, a curry is a perfect main dish to lend an exotic spin to any meal.

tips ■ use cheaper meat cuts if you have the time to cook a curry a long while; go for the more tender (and expensive) cuts if time is of the essence ■ many curries benefit from being cooked one day and eaten the next, allowing the flavours to meld into an aromatic whole overnight ■ store dried spices in airtight containers in the refrigerator or freezer to maintain freshness; freeze any remaining curry pastes for future use ■ there is no need to separate the seeds from a cardamom pod: simply crush the husk with the side of a heavy knife to expose the seeds. Some cooks remove the husks just before serving, but it's not mandatory.

soups

spiced coriander, lentil and barley soup

1 tablespoon coriander seeds

1 tablespoon cumin seeds

1 tablespoon ghee

6 cloves garlic, crushed

2 fresh small red thai chillies, chopped finely

1¼ cups (250g) soup mix

1 litre (4 cups) chicken stock

3½ cups (875ml) water

1 cup coarsely chopped fresh coriander

⅓ cup (95g) greek-style yogurt

1 tablespoon mango chutney

preparation time 10 minutes (plus cooling time)
▦ cooking time 1 hour 20 minutes ▦ serves 4

1 Dry-fry seeds in large saucepan, stirring, until fragrant. Using pestle and mortar, crush seeds.

2 Melt ghee in same pan; cook crushed seeds, garlic and chilli, stirring, 5 minutes.

3 Add soup mix, stock and the water; bring to a boil. Reduce heat; simmer, covered, stirring occasionally, 1 hour. Cool 15 minutes.

4 Blend or process half the soup, in batches, until smooth. Return pureed soup to pan with unprocessed soup; stir over medium heat until hot. Remove from heat; stir in coriander.

5 Serve bowls of soup topped with yogurt and chutney.

tips soup mix, available from supermarkets, is a packaged blend of various dried pulses and grains, among them, lentils, split peas and barley

roasted tomato and pepper soup

2 large red peppers (700g)

5 large vine-ripened tomatoes (1.2kg), halved

1 tablespoon olive oil

1 medium brown onion (150g), chopped coarsely

2 cloves garlic, crushed

4 fresh long red chillies, chopped coarsely

2 cups (500ml) water

2 cups (500ml) vegetable stock

cooking-oil spray

2 tablespoons sour cream

2 tablespoons finely chopped fresh chives

preparation time 20 minutes ▓ cooking time 35 minutes ▓ serves 4

1 Preheat oven to very hot (240°C/220°C fan-assisted).

2 Quarter peppers, discard seeds and membranes. Roast peppers, skin-side up, and tomato, cut-side up, on lightly oiled oven trays, uncovered, about 15 minutes or until pepper skin blisters and blackens and tomato softens. Cover pepper pieces with plastic or paper for 5 minutes; peel away skin, cover to keep warm. Cool tomato 5 minutes; peel away skin.

3 Heat oil in large saucepan; cook onion, garlic and chilli, stirring, until onion softens. Add pepper and tomato; cook, stirring, 5 minutes. Add the water and stock. Bring to a boil then reduce heat; simmer, uncovered, 10 minutes.

4 Blend or process tomato mixture, in batches, until smooth. Pass through fine sieve into large saucepan; discard solids.

5 Divide soup among serving bowls; top with sour cream and chives. Serve with toasted tortilla strips, if desired.

algerian chicken and chickpea soup

2 tablespoons olive oil

350g chicken breast fillets

1 large brown onion (200g), chopped finely

2 cloves garlic, crushed

4cm piece fresh ginger (20g), grated

1½ teaspoons ground cumin

1½ teaspoons ground coriander

1 teaspoon ground turmeric

½ teaspoon sweet paprika

1 cinnamon stick

¼ cup (35g) plain flour

1 litre (4 cups) chicken stock

1 litre (4 cups) water

2 x 300g cans chickpeas, rinsed, drained

2 x 400g cans crushed tomatoes

2 tablespoons finely chopped preserved lemon

1 tablespoon coarsely chopped fresh coriander

preparation time 20 minutes ▓ cooking time 50 minutes ▓ serves 6

1 Heat half the oil in large frying pan; cook chicken, uncovered, about 10 minutes or until browned both sides and cooked through. Cool; shred chicken coarsely.

2 Heat remaining oil in large saucepan; cook onion, garlic and ginger, stirring, until onion softens. Add spices; cook, stirring, until fragrant.

3 Add flour; cook, stirring, until mixture bubbles and thickens. Gradually stir in stock and the water; cook, stirring, until mixture comes to a boil. Simmer, uncovered, 20 minutes.

4 Add chickpeas and undrained tomatoes, bring to a boil; simmer, uncovered, 10 minutes.

5 Add chicken and lemon; stir soup over heat until hot. Just before serving, stir in fresh coriander.

Gumbo, an African word for okra, is basically any Cajun soup thickened with a roux (a flour/butter mix), usually including rice and sausage. Okra, introduced to creole-cajun cooking by African slaves brought to Louisiana, is a distinctively textured green vegetable often used in casseroles, stews and soups.

chicken, chorizo and okra gumbo

3 litres (12 cups) water

1.5kg whole chicken

2 medium carrots (240g), chopped coarsely

2 trimmed celery stalks (200g), chopped coarsely

1 medium brown onion (150g), chopped coarsely

12 black peppercorns

1 bay leaf

60g butter

1 small brown onion (80g), chopped finely, extra

2 cloves garlic, crushed

1 medium red pepper (200g), chopped finely

2 teaspoons dried oregano

1 teaspoon sweet paprika

¼ teaspoon cayenne pepper

¼ teaspoon ground clove

¼ cup (35g) plain flour

¼ cup (70g) tomato paste

400g can crushed tomatoes

100g fresh okra, halved diagonally

1 cup (200g) long grain rice

1 chorizo sausage (170g), sliced thinly

preparation time 30 minutes ▍ cooking time 2 hours 45 minutes ▍ serves 8

1 Place the water in large saucepan with chicken, carrot, celery, onion, peppercorns and bay leaf; bring to a boil. Reduce heat; simmer, covered, 1½ hours.

2 Remove chicken from pan. Strain broth through muslin-lined sieve or colander into large heatproof bowl; discard solids. When chicken is cool enough to handle, remove and discard skin and bones; shred meat coarsely.

3 Melt butter in large saucepan; cook extra onion and garlic, stirring, until onion softens. Add pepper, herbs and spices; cook, stirring, until mixture is fragrant. Add flour and paste; cook, stirring, 1 minute. Gradually stir in reserved broth and undrained tomatoes; bring to a boil, stirring. Stir in okra and rice, reduce heat; simmer, uncovered, about 15 minutes, stirring occasionally, or until rice is tender.

4 Meanwhile, heat large oiled frying pan; cook sausage until browned; drain. Add sausage with chicken to gumbo; stir over medium heat until hot.

tips if you cook this soup a day ahead, the flavours will meld, making it even more delicious – follow the recipe to the end of step 2 then cool the soup, cover and refrigerate it overnight

curried cauliflower soup

1 tablespoon olive oil

1 medium brown onion (150g),
chopped finely

2 cloves garlic, crushed

½ cup (150g) mild curry paste

2 litres (8 cups) water

1 small cauliflower (1kg), trimmed,
chopped coarsely

2 medium potatoes (400g), chopped
coarsely

1 tablespoon tomato paste

1 cup (250ml) buttermilk

½ cup loosely packed fresh coriander
leaves

preparation time 20 minutes (plus cooling time)
▌ cooking time 25 minutes ▌ serves 6

1 Heat oil in large saucepan; cook onion and garlic, stirring, until
onion softens. Add curry paste; cook, stirring, 5 minutes.

2 Add the water, cauliflower, potato and paste; bring to a boil.
Reduce heat; simmer, uncovered, about 15 minutes or until
vegetables are tender. Cool 15 minutes.

3 Blend or process soup, in batches, until smooth. Return soup to
same cleaned pan, add buttermilk; stir over low heat until hot.

4 Serve bowls of soup sprinkled with coriander and, if desired,
accompanied with warmed naan bread.

curry and lime lentil soup

2 teaspoons vegetable oil

1 tablespoon hot curry paste

1 medium brown onion (150g), chopped finely

2 cloves garlic, crushed

2cm piece fresh ginger (10g), grated

1 teaspoon cumin seeds

1 cup (200g) red lentils

2 cups (500ml) vegetable stock

2½ cups (625ml) water

400g can diced tomatoes

1 teaspoon finely grated lime rind

¼ cup (60ml) lime juice

⅓ cup finely chopped fresh flat-leaf parsley

preparation time 15 minutes ▦ cooking time 30 minutes ▦ serves 4

1 Heat oil in large saucepan; cook curry paste, stirring, until fragrant. Add onion, garlic, ginger and cumin; cook, stirring, until onion softens.

2 Add lentils, stock, the water and undrained tomatoes. Bring to a boil; reduce heat. Simmer, uncovered, about 20 minutes or until lentils are softened.

3 Stir in rind and juice; return to a boil. Remove from heat; stir in parsley.

Traditionally, black bean soup is served with small bowls of complementary condiments such as chopped hard-boiled egg, sour cream, paper-thin slices of red onion, lime wedges and chilli and chopped coriander leaves. Diners help themselves to whatever flavours they want to stir into their soup.

cuban black bean soup

2½ cups (500g) dried black beans

1kg ham bone

¼ cup (60ml) olive oil

2 medium brown onions (300g), chopped finely

1 medium red pepper (200g), chopped finely

4 cloves garlic, crushed

1 tablespoon ground cumin

1 teaspoon dried chilli flakes

400g can chopped tomatoes

2.5 litres (10 cups) water

1 tablespoon dried oregano

2 teaspoons ground black pepper

¼ cup (60ml) lime juice

2 medium tomatoes (300g), chopped finely

¼ cup coarsely chopped fresh coriander

2 limes, quartered

preparation time 30 minutes (plus standing time)
▥ cooking time 2 hours 15 minutes ▥ serves 8

1 Place beans in medium bowl, cover with water, stand overnight; drain. Rinse under cold water; drain.

2 Preheat oven to 220°C/200°C fan-assisted.

3 Roast ham bone on oven tray, uncovered, 30 minutes.

4 Meanwhile, heat oil in large saucepan; cook onion, pepper and garlic, stirring, until vegetables soften. Add cumin and chilli; cook, stirring, 1 minute. Add beans and ham bone to pan with undrained canned tomatoes, the water, oregano and pepper; bring to a boil. Reduce heat; simmer, uncovered, 1½ hours.

5 Remove ham bone from soup. When cool enough to handle, remove ham from bone, shred coarsely. Discard the bone.

6 Return ham to soup; bring to a boil. Reduce heat, simmer, uncovered, until soup is hot. Remove from heat; stir in juice, fresh tomato and coriander.

7 Serve bowls of soup with lime wedges.

tips some Cuban chefs like to mash half the beans then return them to the soup, giving it a smooth, almost velvet-like consistency

salsas

chunky corn and courgette salsa

2 corn cobs (800g), trimmed

100g baby courgettes, halved lengthways

2 large avocados (640g), chopped coarsely

200g cherry tomatoes, halved

1 medium red onion (170g), sliced thickly

¼ cup coarsely chopped fresh coriander

1 tablespoon sweet chilli sauce

⅓ cup (80ml) lime juice

2 fresh small red chillies, sliced thinly

preparation time 20 minutes ▦ cooking time 10 minutes
▦ makes 7 cups

1 Cook corn and courgettes on heated oiled grill plate (or grill
or barbecue) until tender and browned lightly. Using sharp knife,
remove kernels from cobs.
2 Combine corn and courgettes in large bowl with avocado,
tomato, onion and coriander. Add remaining ingredients; toss
gently to combine.

tips goes well with
pork ribs and marinated
spatchcock chicken

chile con queso

preparation time 10 minutes ▓ cooking time 10 minutes ▓ makes 2 cups

2 teaspoons vegetable oil
½ small green pepper (75g), chopped finely
½ small brown onion (40g), chopped finely
1 tablespoon pickled jalapeño chillies, chopped finely
1 clove garlic, crushed
½ x 400g can undrained chopped tomatoes
250g cream cheese, softened

1 Heat oil in medium saucepan; cook pepper, onion, chilli and garlic, stirring, until onion softens. Add tomato; cook, stirring, 2 minutes.
2 Add cheese; whisk until cheese melts and dip is smooth.
3 Serve hot with corn chips, if desired.

guacamole

preparation time 10 minutes ▮ makes 2½ cups

2 medium avocados (500g)
½ small red onion (50g), chopped finely
1 medium plum tomato (75g), deseeded, chopped finely
1 tablespoon lime juice
¼ cup coarsely chopped fresh coriander

1 Mash avocados in medium bowl; stir in remaining ingredients.

tips goes well with nachos, burritos and fajitas

salsa fresca

preparation time 20 minutes ▥ makes 1 cup

½ cup finely chopped fresh flat-leaf parsley
¼ cup finely chopped fresh dill
¼ cup finely chopped fresh chives
1 tablespoon wholegrain mustard
2 tablespoons lemon juice
2 tablespoons drained, rinsed baby capers, chopped finely
1 clove garlic, crushed
⅓ cup (80ml) olive oil

1 Combine ingredients in small bowl.

tips goes well with grilled lamb; pork chops

mango and avocado salsa

preparation time 15 minutes ▮ makes 2½ cups

1 medium mango (430g), chopped coarsely
1 large avocado (320g), chopped coarsely
1 small red onion (100g), chopped finely
1 small red pepper (150g), chopped finely
1 fresh small red chilli, chopped finely
2 tablespoons lime juice

tips goes well with roasted
sweet corn, red onion and black bean
salad; grilled salmon fillets

1 Combine ingredients in medium bowl.

corn and tomato relish

2 x 400g cans diced tomatoes
1 medium red pepper (200g),
chopped finely
1 large brown onion (200g), sliced thinly
1 teaspoon salt
1 cup (220g) white sugar
1 cup (250ml) white wine vinegar
1½ tablespoons mustard powder
420g can corn kernels, drained
2 tablespoons cornflour
1 tablespoon water

preparation time 15 minutes ▓ cooking time 1 hour 30 minutes
▓ makes 4 cups

1 Combine undrained tomatoes, pepper, onion, salt, sugar, vinegar
and mustard powder in medium pan. Bring to the boil then reduce
heat; simmer, uncovered, 1 hour, stirring occasionally. Add corn;
simmer, uncovered, a further 20 minutes.
2 Blend cornflour and the water in small bowl to form a smooth
paste; stir into corn mixture. Bring to a boil then reduce heat;
simmer, uncovered, about 5 minutes or until thickened slightly.
3 Transfer mixture to hot, sterilised jars; seal. Allow to cool, then
refrigerate until required.

tips goes well
with cold meats

tomato and chilli
and raisin relish

4 large tomatoes (880g), peeled,
chopped coarsely
1 medium brown onion (150g),
chopped coarsely
½ cup (110g) firmly packed
brown sugar
1 cup (250ml) white wine vinegar
1 tablespoon ground ginger
1 medium green apple (150g),
chopped coarsely
½ cup (85g) raisins
1 teaspoon dried chilli flakes
1 teaspoon cracked black pepper
2 tablespoons tomato paste

preparation time 15 minutes ▦ cooking time 1 hour 10 minutes
▦ makes 2 cups

1 Combine ingredients in large saucepan; bring to a boil, stirring.
Reduce heat; simmer, uncovered, stirring occasionally, about 1
hour or until relish thickens.
2 Transfer mixture to hot, sterilised jars; seal. Allow to cool, then
refrigerate until required.

tips goes well with
grilled lamb chops;
corn chips

meat & poultry

aromatic vietnamese beef curry

2 tablespoons peanut oil

800g beef strips

1 medium brown onion (150g), chopped finely

3 cloves garlic, crushed

1 fresh long red chilli, chopped finely

10cm stick (20g) fresh Lemongrass, chopped finely

1 star anise

1 cinnamon stick

4 cardamom pods, bruised

350g green beans, cut in 4cm lengths

2 tablespoons ground bean sauce

2 tablespoons fish sauce

½ cup coarsely chopped fresh coriander

½ cup (40g) toasted almond flakes

preparation time 15 minutes ▮ cooking time 20 minutes ▮ serves 4

1 Heat half of the oil in wok; stir-fry beef, in batches, until browned. Cover to keep warm.

2 Heat remaining oil in wok; stir-fry onion until soft. Add garlic, chilli, lemongrass, star anise, cinnamon, cardamom and beans; stir-fry until beans are tender. Discard star anise, cinnamon and cardamom. Return beef to wok with sauces; stir-fry until heated through. Stir in coriander and nuts off the heat.

Modern Vietnamese cuisine reflects the influence of the country's previous French colonists, whereas the traditional food of the people has more in common with neighbouring Chinese dishes. One distinguishing note, however, is that the Vietnamese use fish sauce extensively while Chinese cooking relies more on the presence of soy sauce.

chilli-poached beef
with fresh corn salsa

4 chipotle chillies

⅓ cup (80ml) boiling water

1 medium red onion (150g),
chopped coarsely

2 cups (500ml) water, extra

1 tablespoon ground cumin

1 cup (250ml) beef stock

300g piece beef eye fillet,
cut into 3-mm slices

2 tablespoons sour cream

½ cup coarsely chopped fresh
coriander

fresh corn salsa

1 medium red onion (150g),
chopped coarsely

4 cups (660g) fresh corn kernels

2 cloves garlic, crushed

⅓ cup (80ml) lime juice

3 long green chillies, sliced thinly

1 small avocado (200g), chopped
coarsely

preparation time 25 minutes ▦ cooking time 20 minutes
▦ serves 4

1 Soak chillies in the boiling water in small heatproof bowl for
10 minutes. When cool enough to handle, remove stalks from
chillies; reserve chillies and liquid.

2 Meanwhile, make fresh corn salsa.

3 Cook onion in lightly oiled large frying pan, stirring, until
softened. Add the extra water, cumin, stock, chillies and reserved
liquid. Bring to a boil then reduce heat; simmer, uncovered,
10 minutes. Using slotted spoon, remove solids from chilli
poaching liquid; reserve.

4 Place beef, in single layer, in chilli poaching liquid; turn off heat.
Turn beef over; using slotted spoon, remove beef from liquid after
30 seconds. Cover to keep warm.

5 Blend or process reserved solids with cream until almost
Smooth. Serve beef on salsa; top with chilli cream sauce and
sprinkle with coriander.

▦ **fresh corn salsa** Combine all the ingredients together in
medium bowl.

The food of Trinidad (an island in the southeast Caribbean off the coast of Venezuela) was developed by the influence of East Indian and African cultures, whose people had been brought in to work in the local plantations as slaves. It is identified by its deep, rich spicing, rather than any excessive heat from chillies.

trinidadian beef

2 tablespoons coriander seeds

2 tablespoons cumin seeds

½ teaspoon fennel seeds

½ teaspoon black mustard seeds

½ teaspoon fenugreek seeds

1 teaspoon black peppercorns

1 medium brown onion (150g), chopped finely

2 cloves garlic, quartered

¼ cup coarsely chopped fresh coriander

1 tablespoon fresh thyme leaves

3 fresh small red thai chillies, chopped coarsely

½ teaspoon ground ginger

2 tablespoons coarsely chopped fresh flat-leaf parsley

⅓ cup (80ml) peanut oil

1kg braising beef, cut into 3cm pieces

3 cloves garlic, crushed

1 tablespoon hot curry powder

3 cups (750ml) beef stock

2 fresh small red thai chillies, sliced thinly

preparation time 25 minutes (plus refrigeration time) ▓ cooking time 2 hours 15 minutes ▓ serves 4

1 Dry-fry seeds and peppercorns in small frying pan, stirring, about 1 minute or until fragrant. Crush mixture using mortar and pestle.

2 Blend or process onion, quartered garlic, coriander, thyme, chopped chilli, ginger, parsley and 1 tablespoon of the oil until mixture forms a paste. Transfer curry paste to large bowl; add beef, turn to coat in paste. Cover; refrigerate 30 minutes.

3 Heat remaining oil in large saucepan; cook crushed garlic and curry powder, stirring, 1 minute. Add beef mixture; cook, stirring, over medium heat 10 minutes. Add stock and crushed spice mixture; simmer, covered, 1 hour. Uncover; simmer about 1 hour, stirring occasionally, or until meat is tender and sauce thickens slightly. Serve curry sprinkled with sliced chilli.

beef burritos

preparation time 20 minutes
▓ cooking time 35 minutes ▓ serves 4

1 tablespoon olive oil

500g minced beef

1 medium brown onion (150g), chopped finely

1 clove garlic, crushed

1 teaspoon ground cumin

¼ teaspoon chilli powder

400g can crushed tomatoes

½ cup (125ml) water

300g can kidney beans, rinsed, drained

4 large flour tortillas

1 cup (125g) coarsely grated cheddar

1 teaspoon hot paprika

¾ cup (180g) sour cream

1 tablespoon chopped fresh coriander

1 Heat oil in medium frying pan; cook beef, stirring, until browned. Add onion, garlic and spices; cook, stirring, until onion softens. Stir in undrained crushed tomatoes, the water and beans; simmer, uncovered, about 15 minutes or until mixture thickens.

2 Preheat oven to moderately hot 200°C/ 180°C fan-assisted).

3 Divide warm beef filling among tortillas, roll; secure with toothpicks.

4 Place filled tortillas on oiled oven tray; sprinkle with cheese and paprika. Bake about 10 minutes or until heated through. Remove toothpicks; serve topped with sour cream, coriander and, if desired, guacamole (see page 19).

chile con carne

1 tablespoon olive oil

1 large brown onion (200g), chopped finely

1 clove garlic, crushed

2 fresh long red chillies, chopped finely

500g minced beef

2 x 400g cans chopped tomatoes

⅓ cup (90g) tomato paste

½ teaspoon cayenne pepper

2 teaspoons white sugar

1 cup (250ml) beef stock

420g can red kidney beans, rinsed, drained

preparation time 10 minutes ▓ cooking time 45 minutes ▓ serves 4

1 Heat oil in large saucepan; cook onion, garlic and chilli, stirring, until onion softens. Add mince; cook, stirring, over medium heat until mince is browned lightly.

2 Add tomatoes with their juice, paste, cayenne pepper, sugar and stock. Bring to boil then reduce heat; simmer, uncovered, stirring occasionally, about 25 minutes or until most of the liquid has evaporated.

3 Add beans; cook, covered, a further 10 minutes. Serve with toasted flour tortillas, if desired.

South-East Asian food, in general, is a complex affair, having four distinct tastes – sweet, salty, spicy, sour – and a less dominant fifth, bitter. Nowhere do these different flavours meet and blend more harmoniously than in Thai curries such as this one, a perfect amalgam of sweet (coconut cream), salty (fish sauce), spicy (thai red curry paste) and sour (kaffir lime).

thai red beef curry

1 tablespoon peanut oil

4 x 125g fillet steaks

¼ cup (75g) thai red curry paste

225g can bamboo shoots, drained, rinsed

2 x 400ml cans coconut cream

½ cup (125ml) beef stock

2 tablespoons fish sauce

2 tablespoons lime juice

2 fresh kaffir lime leaves, shredded finely

4 large courgettes (600g), sliced thinly

⅓ cup firmly packed fresh thai basil leaves

preparation time 15 minutes ▪ cooking time 1 hour 40 minutes ▪ serves 4

1 Heat oil in large flameproof casserole dish; cook beef, in batches, until well-browned both sides.

2 Cook paste in same dish, stirring, until fragrant. Return beef to dish with bamboo shoots, coconut cream, stock, sauce, juice and lime leaves; simmer, uncovered, 1 hour 20 minutes. Add courgettes, simmer about 5 minutes or until tender.

3 Serve curry sprinkled with basil.

tips add one or two finely chopped fresh red chillies along with the bamboo shoots for some extra heat, if desired

spice-rubbed beef fillet with chickpea and preserved lemon salad

preparation time 20 minutes (plus refrigeration time) ▮ cooking time 15 minutes ▮ serves 4

1 teaspoon coriander seeds
1 teaspoon kalonji seeds (see glossary)
1 teaspoon dried chilli flakes
1 teaspoon sea salt
1 clove garlic, crushed
600g piece beef eye fillet, trimmed
6 large plum tomatoes (540g), peeled
425g can chickpeas, rinsed, drained
2 tablespoons finely chopped preserved lemon rind
⅔ cup loosely packed fresh flat-leaf parsley
⅔ cup loosely packed fresh coriander
1 tablespoon lemon juice

1 Using mortar and pestle, crush seeds, chilli, salt and garlic into coarse paste; rub paste into beef. Cover; refrigerate 20 minutes.
2 Meanwhile, quarter tomatoes; discard seeds and pulp. Chop tomato flesh finely. Combine in medium bowl with chickpeas, rind, herbs and juice.
3 Cook beef on lightly oiled heated grill plate (or grill or barbecue) until brown all over and cooked as desired. Cover; stand 10 minutes. Serve thinly sliced beef on salad.

curried beef
and lentils

preparation time 10 minutes
cooking time 30 minutes ▦ serves 4

½ cup (100g) yellow split peas
2 teaspoons vegetable oil
1 small brown onion (80g), sliced thinly
1 large tomato (220g), chopped coarsely
1 tablespoon curry powder
5 cups bolognese sauce
⅓ cup (55g) raisins
1 loaf turkish bread (430g), quartered
¾ cup (200g) Greek-style yogurt

1 Cook split peas in medium saucepan of boiling
water, uncovered, until just tender; drain.
2 Meanwhile, heat oil in medium frying pan;
cook onion, tomato and curry powder, stirring,
until onion softens. Add split peas, bolognese
sauce and raisins; bring to the boil.
3 Meanwhile, preheat grill. Halve bread quarters
crossways; toast cut sides under grill.
4 Serve beef with toast; top with yogurt.

tips for this recipe, use your favourite
bolognaise sauce recipe – you can even
use leftover sauce ▦ sprinkle with fresh
coriander, if desired.

xacutti

1 cup (80g) desiccated coconut
½ teaspoon ground cinnamon
4 whole cloves
8 dried long red chillies
1 teaspoon ground turmeric
1 tablespoon poppy seeds
1 tablespoon cumin seeds
1 tablespoon fennel seeds
2 tablespoons coriander seeds
2 teaspoons black peppercorns
2 star anise
6 cloves garlic, quartered
2 tablespoons ghee
1 large brown onion (200g), chopped
finely
1kg rump steak, diced
2 cups (500ml) water
2 cups (500ml) beef stock
2 tablespoons lime juice

preparation time 25 minutes cooking time 1 hour 15 minutes
 serves 4

1 Dry-fry coconut in large frying pan over medium heat, stirring,
until browned lightly; remove coconut from pan. Dry-fry cinnamon,
cloves, chillies, turmeric, seeds, peppercorns and star anise in
same pan, stirring, about 1 minute or until fragrant.
2 Blend or process coconut, spice mixture and garlic until fine.
3 Heat ghee in large saucepan; cook onion, stirring, until onion
softens. Add coconut spice mixture; cook, stirring, until fragrant.
Add beef; cook, stirring, about 2 minutes or until beef is coated
with coconut spice mixture.
4 Add the water and stock; simmer, covered, 30 minutes, stirring
occasionally. Uncover; cook 30 minutes or until beef is tender and
sauce thickened slightly. Stir juice into curry off the heat; sprinkle
with fresh sliced chilli if you like.

Xacutti is a Goan curry, not as well known as the vindaloo,
another speciality of the formerly Portuguese, now Indian,
state. Traditionally made with mutton or chicken and a
dry curry paste with fried coconut, it has lime juice added
just before serving, which further distinguishes it from a
vinegary vindaloo.

This recipe showcases the significant influences of neighbouring cuisines on Singaporean cooking. Borrowing culinary techniques from Malaysia, India and China, chillies and spices laced with coconut milk are characteristic of this island nation's food.

meatballs in spicy coconut milk

800g minced beef

2 eggs

2 teaspoons cornflour

2 cloves garlic, crushed

1 tablespoon finely chopped fresh coriander

1 fresh long red chilli, chopped finely

2 purple shallots (50g), chopped coarsely

3 cloves garlic, quartered

1 teaspoon chilli flakes

7 fresh long red chillies, chopped coarsely

2 tablespoons peanut oil

2cm piece fresh galangal (10g), sliced thinly (see glossary)

3 large tomatoes (660g), deseeded, chopped coarsely

400ml can coconut milk

1 tablespoon kecap asin

1 large tomato (220g), deseeded, diced

½ cup (40g) fried shallots

1 fresh small red chilli, sliced thinly

preparation time 25 minutes ▥ cooking time 20 minutes ▥ serves 4

1 Combine mince, eggs, cornflour, crushed garlic, coriander and finely chopped chilli in medium bowl; roll level tablespoons of mixture into balls. Place meatballs, in single layer, in large baking-parchment-lined bamboo steamer. Steam, covered, over wok of simmering water 10 minutes.

2 Meanwhile, blend or process purple shallots, quartered garlic, chilli flakes, coarsely chopped chilli and half of the oil until mixture forms a paste.

3 Heat remaining oil in wok; cook shallot paste and galangal, stirring, about 1 minute or until fragrant. Add chopped tomato; cook, stirring, 1 minute. Add coconut milk, kecap asin and Meatballs; simmer, uncovered, stirring occasionally, about 5 minutes or until meatballs are cooked through and sauce thickens slightly.

4 Serve curry topped with diced tomato, fried shallots and thinly sliced chilli.

tips kecap asin, an astringent, salty soy sauce used in Indonesian cuisine, is available from Asian food stores

beef do-piaza

200g yogurt
¼ teaspoon saffron threads
¼ cup (60ml) vegetable oil
1kg stewing steak, cut into
2cm pieces
2 medium brown onions (300g),
chopped finely
2 teaspoons ground cumin
2 teaspoons coriander seeds
1 teaspoon ground cardamom
1 teaspoon ground fenugreek
½ teaspoon ground turmeric
2 cloves garlic, crushed
2cm piece fresh ginger (10g),
grated
2 long green chillies, sliced thinly
2 x 400g cans crushed tomatoes
1 cup (250ml) beef stock
2 tablespoons peanut oil
2 medium brown onions (300g),
sliced thinly

preparation time 30 minutes ▓ cooking time 2 hours ▓ serves 4

1 Combine yogurt and saffron in small bowl. Set aside.
2 Heat vegetable oil in large flameproof casserole dish; cook beef, in batches, until browned all over.
3 Cook chopped onion in same dish, stirring, until soft. Add spices, garlic, ginger and chilli; cook, stirring, until fragrant. Add undrained tomatoes and stock; bring to a boil. Return beef to dish; simmer, covered, about 1½ hours or until beef is tender. Stir in yogurt mixture.
4 Meanwhile, heat peanut oil in large frying pan; cook sliced onion, stirring, until browned lightly. Sprinkle over curry to serve.

Do-piaza, meaning 'two-onions', is a dish from the Hydrabad region of India and does not refer to the amount of onions used in the recipe but to the way they are separately treated. In this recipe, one onion is chopped finely and one is sliced thinly, giving the dish a unique texture.

Sandwiched between the Middle East and the Indian subcontinent, Afghanistan food has been influenced by the cuisines of all the countries in these areas. In this recipe, its Iranian and Turkish influences are shown by the addition of nutmeg and cinnamon, while the rich, thick sauce from the combined tomato, stock and spinach resemble a traditional Indian curry.

afghani lamb and spinach curry

preparation time 20 minutes ▓ cooking time 1 hour 30 minutes
▓ serves 4

1½ tablespoons vegetable oil

1kg lamb shoulder, trimmed, diced into 3cm pieces

1 large brown onion (200g), chopped finely

4 cloves garlic, crushed

2 teaspoons ground turmeric

½ teaspoon ground nutmeg

½ teaspoon ground cinnamon

½ teaspoon cayenne pepper

400g can chopped tomatoes

2 cups (500ml) beef stock

350g fresh spinach

1 tablespoon finely grated lemon rind

⅓ cup (45g) toasted slivered almonds

1 Heat half the oil in large saucepan; cook lamb, in batches, until browned all over.

2 Heat remaining oil in same pan; cook onion, garlic and spices, stirring, until onion softens.

3 Add lamb, undrained tomatoes and stock; simmer, covered, about 1 hour. Uncover; simmer 15 minutes or until sauce thickens and lamb is tender. Add spinach and rind; stir over heat about 1 minute or until spinach wilts. Serve curry sprinkled with almonds.

Stoba, a popular stew eaten throughout the islands of the Caribbean, is usually made with goat's meat, but we've used lamb because it's easier to find. If you can get goat, however, do try this recipe using a kilo of any trimmed cubed cut of meat.

lamb stoba

preparation time 10 minutes ▦ cooking time 1 hour 30 minutes ▦ serves 4

2 tablespoons vegetable oil

1kg lamb shoulder, trimmed, diced into 3cm pieces

2 medium brown onions (300g), sliced thinly

3cm piece fresh ginger (15g), sliced thinly

2 fresh long red chillies, sliced thinly

1 medium red pepper (200g), chopped coarsely

2 teaspoons ground cumin

2 teaspoons ground allspice

1 cinnamon stick

2 x 400g cans chopped tomatoes

2 teaspoons finely grated lime rind

2 tablespoons lime juice

¼ cup (55g) firmly packed brown sugar

1 Heat half the oil in large saucepan; cook lamb, in batches, until browned all over.

2 Heat remaining oil in same pan; cook onion, ginger, chilli, Pepper and spices, stirring, until onion softens.

3 Add lamb and remaining ingredients; simmer, covered, about 1 hour or until lamb is tender.

rogan josh

preparation time 25 minutes ▮ cooking time
1 hour 50 minutes ▮ serves 6

1 tablespoon vegetable oil

1kg lamb shoulder, diced into 3cm pieces

3 medium brown onions (450g), sliced thinly

4cm piece fresh ginger (20g), grated

2 cloves garlic, crushed

⅔ cup (200g) prepared rogan josh paste

1½ cups (375ml) water

425g can diced tomatoes

1 cinnamon stick

5 cardamom pods, bruised

2 tablespoons coarsely chopped fresh coriander

1 Heat half the oil in large saucepan; cook lamb, in batches, until browned.

2 Heat remaining oil in same pan; cook onion, stirring, until soft. Add ginger, garlic and paste; cook, stirring, until fragrant.

3 Return lamb to pan; stir to combine with paste mixture. Add the water, undrained tomatoes, cinnamon and cardamom; simmer, covered, about 1½ hours or until lamb is tender. Serve curry sprinkled with coriander.

Rogan josh, made traditionally with lamb, is an Indian tomato-based curry, and literally means 'meat in spicy red sauce'. It is slightly milder than many curries due in equal part to the fairly large amount of tomato used and the very little chilli found in the paste.

Keema is minced meat, usually beef or lamb, and is the meat found in samosas. Here, our subtle, yet fragrant, curry is fairly dry, not unlike a bolognese sauce, and can be eaten in the hand, picked up by pieces of roti or naan. Cooked down further, it can be treated as a filling for 'pan rolls', an Indian version of a crépe that, once stuffed, is crumbed and shallow-fried.

keema with green chilli and tomato

2 tablespoons ghee
1 medium brown onion (150g), chopped finely
5cm piece fresh ginger (25g), grated
2 cloves garlic, crushed
3 long green chillies, chopped finely
2 teaspoons cumin seeds
2 teaspoons ground coriander
1 teaspoon ground turmeric
2 teaspoons garam masala (see page 50)
800g minced lamb
400g can chopped tomatoes
2 large tomatoes (440g), chopped coarsely
⅓ cup (95g) plain yogurt
1 tablespoon lemon juice
1 cup (120g) frozen peas
2 tablespoons coarsely chopped fresh coriander

preparation time 20 minutes ▓ cooking time 45 minutes
▓ serves 4

1 Heat ghee in large saucepan; cook onion, ginger, garlic and two-thirds of the chilli, stirring, until onion softens. Add spices; cook, stirring, until fragrant. Add mince; cook, stirring, until mince changes colour.
2 Add undrained tomatoes and fresh tomato; cook, stirring occasionally, about 15 minutes or until mince is cooked through and sauce has thickened.
3 Add remaining chilli, yogurt, juice and peas; cook, uncovered, until peas are just tender. Serve curry sprinkled with coriander.

nepalese meatball curry

2 tablespoons vegetable oil

1 small white onion (80g), chopped finely

3 cloves garlic, crushed

5cm piece fresh ginger (25g), grated

750g minced lamb

1 egg

1 egg yolk

1 fresh long red chilli, chopped finely

1 teaspoon ground cumin

½ teaspoon ground turmeric

¼ cup coarsely chopped fresh coriander

2 tablespoons stale breadcrumbs

¼ cup (60ml) lemon juice

curry sauce

1 tablespoon vegetable oil

1 medium white onion (150g),
chopped finely

1 clove garlic, crushed

3cm piece fresh ginger (15g), grated

1 tablespoon coarsely chopped coriander
root and stem mixture

2 teaspoons ground cumin

1 teaspoon ground fenugreek

1 teaspoon yellow mustard seeds

1 teaspoon ground turmeric

2 x 400g cans crushed tomatoes

1 cup (250ml) beef stock

preparation time 30 minutes ▓ cooking time 1 hour 20 minutes
▓ serves 4

1 Make curry sauce.

2 Meanwhile, heat half of the oil in large frying pan; cook onion, garlic and ginger, stirring, until onion softens. Cool 10 minutes.

3 Combine minced lamb, whole egg and yolk, chilli, spices, coriander, breadcrumbs and onion mixture in large bowl; roll level tablespoons of the lamb mixture into balls.

4 Heat remaining oil in same pan; cook meatballs, in batches, until browned all over.

5 Add meatballs to curry sauce; cook, uncovered, about 20 minutes or until meatballs are cooked through. Stir juice into curry off the heat.

▓ curry sauce Heat oil in large saucepan; cook onion, garlic and ginger, stirring, until onion softens. Add coriander mixture and spices; cook, stirring, until fragrant. Add undrained tomatoes and stock; simmer, covered, 1 hour.

Nepalese food, heavily influenced by the neighbouring countries of India and Tibet, uses mostly lamb in its cooking because, like its neighbour to the south, the country's predominant religion is Hindu, which holds the cow sacred.

This recipe uses black mustard seeds (sometimes sold as brown mustard seeds), which are more pungent than the white (or yellow) seeds used in most prepared mustards.

malaysian lamb curry

1 tablespoon ground cumin

1 tablespoon black mustard seeds

1 teaspoon ground turmeric

1kg diced lamb shoulder

¼ cup (60ml) vegetable oil

2 medium brown onions (300g), sliced thinly

2 cloves garlic, crushed

3 dried long red chillies, chopped coarsely

2 long green chillies, chopped coarsely

400ml can coconut cream

1 cup (250ml) beef stock

200g sugarsnap peas, trimmed

½ cup loosely packed fresh coriander leaves

garam masala

1 tablespoon fennel seeds

2 teaspoons ground cinnamon

1 teaspoon ground cardamom

1 teaspoon cracked black pepper

½ teaspoon ground clove

1 bay leaf

preparation time 20 minutes ▦ cooking time 1 hour 30 minutes ▦ serves 4

1 Make garam masala.

2 Combine spices in large bowl, add lamb; mix well.

3 Heat two tablespoons of the oil in large saucepan; cook lamb mixture, in batches, until browned.

4 Heat remaining oil in same pan; cook onion, garlic and chillies over low heat, stirring, until onion softens.

5 Return lamb to pan with coconut cream and stock; simmer, covered, 1 hour 20 minutes. Uncover, stir in peas off the heat. Serve curry sprinkled with coriander.

▦ garam masala Dry-fry ingredients in small frying pan, stirring until fragrant. Blend or process mixture, or crush using mortar and pestle, until mixture is ground coarsely.

lamb and okra tagine in rich tomato sauce with spiced garlic

preparation time 20 minutes ▓ cooking time 2 hours 10 minutes ▓ serves 4

1 tablespoon olive oil

1kg boned lamb shoulder, trimmed, chopped coarsely

2 medium brown onions (300g), chopped coarsely

7 medium tomatoes (1kg), chopped coarsely

1 litre (4 cups) water

200g okra

½ cup loosely packed fresh mint leaves

spiced garlic

1 teaspoon coriander seeds

½ teaspoon cardamom seeds

30g butter

5 cloves garlic, sliced thinly

1 teaspoon dried chilli flakes

1 teaspoon salt

▓ **spiced garlic** Using mortar and pestle, crush seeds. Melt butter in small saucepan; cook seeds, garlic, chilli and salt over low heat, stirring, about 10 minutes or until garlic softens.

1 Heat oil in large deep saucepan; cook lamb, in batches, until browned all over.

2 Cook onion in same pan, stirring, until soft. Add tomato and the water; bring to a boil. Return lamb to pan; simmer, uncovered, stirring occasionally, about 1¾ hours or until lamb is tender.

3 Add okra to lamb mixture; simmer, uncovered, about 15 minutes or until okra is tender.

4 Meanwhile, make spiced garlic.

5 Serve casserole with spiced garlic, mint and steamed white long-grain rice, if desired.

Harissa, a traditional spice paste from North Africa, can be used in sauces and dressings, as a rub for meat, or eaten on its own as a condiment.

harissa marinated lamb with warm couscous salad

30g dried red chillies, chopped coarsely

1 teaspoon ground cumin

1 teaspoon ground coriander

1 teaspoon caraway seeds

2 cloves garlic, crushed

1 teaspoon salt

1 teaspoon white sugar

⅓ cup (90g) tomato puree

⅓ cup (80ml) olive oil

2kg lamb leg

warm couscous salad

2 small sweet potatoes (500g), diced into 1cm pieces

cooking-oil spray

2 cups (400g) couscous

½ cup (60g) frozen peas, thawed

1 tablespoon finely grated lemon rind

2½ cups (625ml) boiling water

1 small red onion (100g), chopped finely

½ cup finely shredded fresh flat-leaf parsley

¼ cup finely shredded fresh mint

2 tablespoons olive oil

1 tablespoon red wine vinegar

¼ cup (60ml) lemon juice

preparation time 40 minutes (plus standing and refrigeration time)
▓ cooking time 1 hour 5 minutes ▓ serves 4

1 Place chilli in small heatproof bowl, cover with boiling water; stand 1 hour. Drain chilli; reserve ¼ cup of the liquid.

2 Dry-fry cumin, coriander and caraway in heated small frying pan until fragrant. Blend or process spices with chilli, reserved soaking liquid, garlic, salt, sugar and puree until mixture is almost smooth. With motor operating, add oil in a thin, steady stream; process until harissa forms a smooth paste. Reserve ⅓ cup harissa.

3 Using sharp knife, pierce lamb all over; place in large bowl. Rub remaining harissa over lamb, pressing into cuts. Cover; refrigerate 3 hours or overnight.

4 Preheat oven to 200°C/180°C fan-assisted.

5 Pour enough water into large shallow baking dish to come about 5mm up the sides; place lamb on wire rack over dish. Roast, uncovered, about 1 hour or until cooked as desired. Cover lamb; stand 20 minutes then slice thinly.

6 Meanwhile, make warm couscous salad.

7 Serve lamb with salad.

▓ warm couscous salad Place sweet potatoes, in single layer, on oiled oven tray; spray with cooking-oil spray. Roast, uncovered, for last 30 minutes of lamb cooking time. Combine couscous, peas, rind and the water in large heatproof bowl; cover, stand about 5 minutes or until water is absorbed, fluffing with fork occasionally. Stir sweet potatoes, onion, herbs and the combined olive oil, vinegar and juice into couscous salad just before serving.

pork and lemongrass curry

3 x 10cm sticks (60g) fresh
lemongrass, chopped finely
4 cloves garlic, quartered
4cm piece (20g) fresh galangal,
sliced thinly
1 teaspoon ground turmeric
2 fresh jalapeño chillies,
quartered
½ cup (125ml) water
¼ cup (60ml) peanut oil
½ teaspoon shrimp paste
2 x 400ml cans coconut milk
3 fresh kaffir lime leaves, torn
1kg pork fillet, cut into 1cm slices
2 tablespoons lime juice

preparation time 20 minutes ▓ cooking time 45 minutes
▓ serves 4

1 Blend or process lemongrass, garlic, galangal, turmeric and
chilli with the water until mixture forms a paste.
2 Heat 1 tablespoon of the oil in large saucepan; cook lemongrass
paste and shrimp paste, stirring, about 1 minute or until fragrant.
Add coconut milk and lime leaves; simmer, uncovered, about
30 minutes or until sauce thickens slightly.
3 Meanwhile, heat remaining oil in large frying pan and cook
pork, in batches, until browned. Add pork and juice to curry sauce;
simmer, uncovered, about 2 minutes or until pork is cooked.

This curry is of Cambodian origin, a country whose cuisine
borrows flavours from Thailand and Vietnam, two of its
near-neighbours, but is somewhat simpler and more refined.
A close relative of ginger, galangal is an important ingredient
in South-East Asian foods and is commonly called for in
recipes. The flavour is stronger and more intense than that
of ginger, so use it sparingly.

pork vindaloo

preparation time 25 minutes ▮ cooking time
1 hour 50 minutes ▮ serves 4

2 tablespoons ghee
1kg pork shoulder, cut into 3cm pieces
1 large red onion (300g), sliced thinly
½ cup (150g) prepared vindaloo paste
2 cloves garlic, crushed
2 cups (500ml) water
¼ cup (60ml) white vinegar
4 medium potatoes (800g), quartered
2 fresh small red thai chillies, chopped finely
2 fresh long red chillies, sliced thinly

1 Heat ghee in large saucepan; cook pork, in
batches, until browned all over.
2 Cook onion in same pan, stirring, until soft.
Add paste and garlic; cook, stirring, about
1 minute or until fragrant.
3 Return pork to pan with the water and vinegar;
simmer, covered, 50 minutes.
4 Add potato; simmer, uncovered, about
45 minutes or until potato is tender. Stir in
chopped chilli; serve curry sprinkled with thinly
sliced chilli.

The king of curries, the fiery Indian vindaloo,
is from the former Portuguese colony of Goa.
The name is derived from the Portuguese words
for vinegar and garlic, the dish's primary
ingredients. Jars of vindaloo paste are available
in supermarkets.

sour pork curry

Sour curries, easy to make and slow cooking, are considered street food in Bangkok, where they're served with pickles and steamed rice. Street vendors sell inexpensive food to busy workers and provide a colourful source of the aromas and tastes of this unique city. Thai basil, or horapa, is available from greengrocers and Asian supermarkets.

preparation time 30 minutes ▯ cooking time 2 hours 15 minutes ▯ serves 4

1 Heat oil in large flameproof casserole dish; cook pork, uncovered, until browned. Remove from dish.
2 Preheat oven to moderately slow (170°C/150°C fan-assisted).
3 Add paste, coriander mixture, galangal and chillies to same dish; cook, stirring, until fragrant. Add sauce, tamarind, sugar, stock and the water; bring to a boil. Return pork to dish, cover; cook in oven 1 hour. Uncover; cook 1 hour.
4 Remove pork from dish, cover; stand 10 minutes before slicing thickly. Stir basil into curry sauce off the heat.

1 tablespoon vegetable oil

1kg pork neck

1 teaspoon shrimp paste

¼ cup coarsely chopped coriander root and stem mixture

2cm piece fresh galangal (10g), chopped finely

5 dried long red chillies, chopped finely

3 fresh long red chillies, chopped finely

2 tablespoons fish sauce

¾ cup (235g) tamarind concentrate

2 tablespoons caster sugar

2 cups (500ml) chicken stock

1 litre (4 cups) water

½ cup fresh thai basil leaves, chopped coarsely

Cambodian food uses techniques and ingredients from Chinese, Indian and Thai cooking, but distils them into an individual style. This recipe smacks of Indian influence, but it's individualised with native ingredients and flavours such as tamarind, the tangy-tasting dried pod of the tamarind tree.

tamarind and citrus pork curry

70g dried tamarind, chopped coarsely

¾ cup (180ml) boiling water

1 tablespoon peanut oil

1 large red onion (300g), chopped finely

1 fresh long red chilli, sliced thinly

5cm piece fresh ginger (25g), grated

2 cloves garlic, crushed

10 fresh curry leaves

2 teaspoons fenugreek seeds

½ teaspoon ground turmeric

1 teaspoon ground coriander

1 teaspoon finely grated lime rind

1 tablespoon lime juice

400ml can coconut cream

6 baby aubergines (360g), chopped coarsely

1kg pork fillet, cut into 2cm dice

preparation time 20 minutes (plus standing time)
cooking time 50 minutes ▓ serves 4

1 Soak tamarind in the boiling water for 30 minutes. Place fine sieve over small bowl; push tamarind through sieve. Discard solids in sieve; reserve pulp in bowl.
2 Heat oil in large saucepan; cook onion, chilli, ginger, garlic, curry leaves, seeds and spices, stirring, until onion softens.
3 Add pulp, rind, juice, coconut cream and aubergines; simmer, covered, 20 minutes. Add pork; simmer, uncovered, about 20 minutes or until pork is cooked.

Sri Lanka, the small island nation at the southern-most tip of India, was occupied by a large number of different cultures in the past, and it is probably due to the Dutch and English that pork remains one of its most popular meats. This curry is typically cooked with the fat left on, to give the dish a deep richness of flavour tempered by the astringency of the vinegar and tamarind.

sri lankan fried pork curry

2 tablespoons vegetable oil

20 fresh curry leaves

½ teaspoon fenugreek seeds

1 large brown onion (200g), chopped finely

4 cloves garlic, crushed

3cm piece fresh ginger (15g), grated

1 tablespoon curry powder

2 teaspoons cayenne pepper

1kg pork belly, chopped coarsely

1 tablespoon white wine vinegar

2 tablespoons tamarind concentrate

1 cinnamon stick

4 cardamom pods, bruised

1½ cups (375ml) water

400ml can coconut milk

preparation time 20 minutes ▓ cooking time 1 hour 20 minutes ▓ serves 4

1 Heat half the oil in large saucepan; cook leaves and seeds until seeds pop and mixture is fragrant. Add onion, garlic and ginger; cook, stirring, until onion softens.

2 Add curry powder and cayenne to pan, then pork; stir well to combine. Add vinegar, tamarind, cinnamon, cardamom and the water; simmer, covered, 1 hour.

3 Heat remaining oil in large frying pan. Transfer pork to pan; cook, stirring, until pork is browned and crisp.

4 Meanwhile, add coconut milk to curry sauce; simmer, stirring, about 5 minutes or until curry thickens slightly. Return pork to curry; stir to combine.

coriander and chilli grilled chicken fillets

preparation time 10 minutes ▓ cooking time 15 minutes ▓ serves 4

6 chicken thigh fillets (660g), halved

chickpea salad

2 x 300g cans chickpeas, rinsed and
drained

2 medium plum tomatoes (150g),
chopped coarsely

2 spring onions, chopped finely

2 tablespoons lime juice

1 cup coarsely chopped fresh coriander

1 tablespoon olive oil

coriander chilli sauce

8 spring onions, chopped coarsely

3 cloves garlic, quartered

3 fresh small red chillies,
chopped coarsely

¼ cup loosely packed fresh coriander
leaves

1 teaspoon white sugar

1 tablespoon fish sauce

¼ cup (60ml) lime juice

1 Make coriander chilli sauce.

2 Cook chicken, in batches, on heated oiled grill plate (or grill or barbecue) until almost cooked through. Brush about two-thirds of the coriander chilli sauce all over chicken; cook further 5 minutes or until chicken is cooked through.

3 Meanwhile, combine ingredients for chickpea salad in large bowl; toss gently.

4 Serve chickpea salad with chicken; sprinkle with remaining coriander chilli sauce.

▓ coriander chilli sauce Blend or process onion, garlic, chilli, coriander and sugar until finely chopped. Add sauce and juice; blend until well combined.

marinated chilli poussins

preparation time 20 minutes (plus refrigeration time) ▮ cooking time 1 hour ▮ serves 8

8 fresh long red chillies
8 cloves garlic, peeled
2 small brown onions (200g),
chopped coarsely
⅓ cup (80ml) red wine vinegar
1 tablespoon ground cumin
2 tablespoons olive oil
4 medium ripe tomatoes (750g),
quartered
4 x 500g poussins

tips a poussin is a small chicken, which is no more than 6 weeks old and weighs a maximum of 500g (see glossary)
▮ serve poussins with remaining chilli sauce and chunky corn and courgette salsa (see page 16)

1 Combine chillies, garlic, onion, vinegar and cumin in food processor; blend until almost smooth.
2 Heat oil in frying pan, add onion mixture; cook, stirring, until fragrant.
3 Process tomatoes until smooth. Add to pan with onion mixture; cook, stirring, until mixture boils. Reduce heat; simmer, uncovered, stirring, about 20 minutes or until thickened. Brush spatchcock chickens with half of chilli sauce; refrigerate 3 hours.
4 Preheat oven to hot (220°C/200°C fan-assisted).
5 Place poussins, skin-side up, on rack in shallow baking dish; roast about 30 minutes or until cooked through.

Green curry paste is one of the hottest Thai traditional pastes, but this doesn't stop it being one of the favourite curries among non-Thai cooks and diners. Here, the coconut milk tempers the fire, but doesn't dilute the beautiful flavour of this curry.

chicken green curry

1 tablespoon peanut oil

¼ cup (75g) green curry paste

3 long green chillies, chopped finely

1kg chicken thigh fillets, cut into 3cm pieces

2 x 400ml cans coconut milk

2 tablespoons fish sauce

2 tablespoons lime juice

1 tablespoon grated palm sugar

150g pea aubergines

1 large courgette (150g), sliced thinly

⅓ cup loosely packed fresh thai basil leaves

¼ cup loosely packed fresh coriander leaves

2 spring onions, chopped coarsely

preparation time 20 minutes ▦ cooking time 30 minutes ▦ serves 4

1 Heat oil in large saucepan; cook paste and about two-thirds of the chilli, stirring, about 2 minutes or until fragrant. Add chicken; cook, stirring, until browned.

2 Add coconut milk, sauce, juice, sugar and aubergines; simmer, uncovered, about 10 minutes or until aubergines are just tender.

3 Add courgettes, basil and coriander; simmer, uncovered, until courgettes are just tender.

4 Serve curry sprinkled with remaining chilli and spring onion.

tips you can buy jars of green curry paste in most supermarkets ▦ pea aubergines can be found in Asian supermarkets and specialist greengrocers

lemongrass chicken curry

1 tablespoon vegetable oil
24 chicken drumsticks (1.7kg)
1 medium brown onion (150g),
sliced thinly
3 cloves garlic, crushed
½ teaspoon cracked black pepper
3 x 10cm sticks (60g) fresh
lemongrass, chopped finely
1 long green chilli, chopped finely
¼ cup (75g) mild curry paste
1 tablespoon grated palm sugar
½ cup (125ml) chicken stock
½ cup (125ml) water
1 medium red pepper (200g),
sliced thinly
1 medium carrot (120g), cut into
matchsticks
4 spring onions, sliced thinly

preparation time 25 minutes ▦ cooking time 45 minutes ▦ serves 4

1 Heat oil in large flameproof casserole dish; cook chicken, in batches, until browned. Drain and discard cooking juices.
2 Cook brown onion, garlic, pepper, lemongrass and chilli in same pan, stirring, until onion softens. Add paste; cook, stirring, until fragrant. Return chicken to dish; cook, stirring, 5 minutes.
3 Add sugar, stock and the water; cook, covered, 10 minutes. Uncover; simmer about 10 minutes or until chicken is cooked through. Remove chicken from dish; cover to keep warm. Add pepper and carrot; cook, uncovered, about 5 minutes or until curry sauce thickens and vegetables are just tender. Stir spring onion into curry off the heat.
4 Serve chicken topped with curried vegetable mixture.

There are many prepared curry pastes sold in supermarkets, but they vary in flavour, heat and intensity from maker to maker. By and large, a rule of thumb is that the milder ones are most likely to be called korma, tikka, panang or yellow; medium pastes can be labelled balti, tandoori, rogan josh, leang or red; while the hotter versions are sold as vindaloo, madras, extra hot, green or crying tiger.

kenyan chicken curry

preparation time 30 minutes (plus refrigeration time) ▓ cooking time 30 minutes ▓ serves 6

8cm piece fresh ginger (40g), grated

6 cloves garlic, crushed

2 teaspoons ground turmeric

½ cup (125ml) lemon juice

⅓ cup (80ml) vegetable oil

1 teaspoon ground cumin

3 teaspoons garam masala (see page 50)

1 tablespoon ground coriander

1 teaspoon paprika

1 teaspoon chilli flakes

¼ cup (70g) yogurt

1kg chicken thigh fillets, cut into

3cm pieces

3 large brown onions (600g), chopped

coarsely

2 teaspoons chilli powder

2 teaspoons ground fenugreek

2 x 400g cans crushed tomatoes

1 stick cinnamon

2 long green chillies, chopped finely

300ml single cream

1 tablespoon honey

¼ cup coarsely chopped fresh coriander

1 Combine half the ginger, half the garlic, half the turmeric, half the juice and half the oil in large bowl with all the cumin, garam masala, ground coriander, paprika, chilli flakes and yogurt, add chicken; turn to coat in marinade. Cover; refrigerate 30 minutes.

2 Preheat oven to very hot (240°C/220°C fan-assisted).

3 Cook chicken, in lightly oiled medium shallow flameproof baking dish, uncovered, 10 minutes.

4 Heat remaining oil in large saucepan; cook onion, chilli powder, fenugreek, remaining ginger, garlic and turmeric, stirring, until onion softens. Add undrained tomatoes, cinnamon, green chilli and remaining juice. Simmer, covered, 10 minutes. Stir in cream and honey; simmer, uncovered, 1 minute.

5 Add chicken to curry; simmer about 5 minutes or until chicken is cooked through. Remove from heat, stir in fresh coriander.

Kenyan cooking is a fusion of East African and Middle Eastern methods known by the name of swahili cooking, a word which identifies the culinary influences of traders arriving by sea from the Arabian peninsula upon the indigenous population. This curry uses the pungency of paprika, coriander and turmeric in the chicken marinade to complement the green chilli and fenugreek in the curry.

mexican chicken stew

preparation time 20 minutes ▓ cooking time 1 hour ▓ serves 4

1 tablespoon vegetable oil

8 chicken drumsticks (1.2kg)

1 large red onion (300g), sliced thickly

2 cloves garlic, crushed

2 fresh long red chillies, chopped finely

1 teaspoon ground cumin

4 medium tomatoes (600g), chopped coarsely

1 cup (250ml) chicken stock

⅓ cup loosely packed fresh oregano leaves

420g can kidney beans, rinsed, drained

1 medium yellow pepper (200g), sliced thickly

1 medium green pepper (200g), sliced thickly

1 Heat half the oil in large saucepan; cook chicken, in batches, until browned all over. Heat remaining oil in pan; cook onion, garlic, chilli and cumin, stirring, until onion softens.

2 Return chicken to pan with tomato, stock and ¼ cup of the oregano; bring to a boil. Reduce heat; simmer, covered, 30 minutes.

3 Add beans and peppers; simmer, uncovered, 20 minutes. Divide stew among bowls; sprinkle with remaining oregano. Serve with sour cream, if liked.

singapore noodles

preparation time 15 minutes ▓ cooking time 10 minutes ▓ serves 4

450g fresh singapore noodles

2 teaspoons sesame oil

2 cloves garlic, crushed

2cm piece fresh ginger (10g), grated

1 medium carrot (120g), cut into matchsticks

250g cooked shelled small prawns

1 tablespoon malaysian curry powder

3 spring onions, sliced thinly

1½ cups bean sprouts (120g)

2 tablespoons soy sauce

¼ cup (60ml) kecap manis (Indonesian sweet soy sauce)

3 cups (480g) shredded barbecued chicken

1 Place noodles in large heatproof bowl; cover with boiling water. Separate noodles with fork; drain.

2 Meanwhile, heat oil in wok; stir-fry garlic, ginger and carrot until carrot is just tender. Add prawns and curry powder; stir-fry until prawns change colour.

3 Add noodles and remaining ingredients; stir-fry until hot.

This curry, also known as opor ayam, is a classic Indonesian dish usually served on special occasions. A good introduction to those unfamiliar with the rich, full-flavoured 'stews' of South-East Asia, the traditional opor ayam is fragrantly spiced without being incendiary.

coconut chicken curry

2 tablespoons vegetable oil

12 chicken drumsticks (1.8kg)

2 tablespoons ground coriander

3 cloves garlic, crushed

5cm piece fresh ginger (25g), grated

10cm stick (20g) fresh lemongrass, chopped finely

10 fresh curry leaves, torn

1 large brown onion (200g), sliced thinly

1 cinnamon stick

2 cardamom pods, bruised

1 tablespoon tamarind concentrate

400g can coconut milk

1 cup (250ml) chicken stock

1 large sweet potato (500g), chopped coarsely

1 clove garlic, chopped finely

2cm piece fresh ginger (10g), chopped finely

1 fresh small red thai chilli, chopped finely

1 long green chilli, chopped finely

¼ cup finely chopped fresh coriander

2 teaspoons finely grated lemon rind

preparation time 30 minutes   cooking time 1 hour 30 minutes   serves 4

1 Heat oil in large deep flameproof casserole dish; cook chicken, in batches, until browned.

2 Cook ground coriander, crushed garlic, ginger, lemongrass and curry leaves in same pan, stirring, until fragrant.

3 Add onion; cook, stirring, about 5 minutes or until onion softens. Return chicken to pan with cinnamon, cardamom, tamarind, coconut milk and stock; simmer, uncovered, 30 minutes.

4 Add sweet potato; simmer, uncovered, 30 minutes or until sweet potato is just tender and chicken is cooked through. Discard cinnamon and cardamom.

5 Meanwhile, combine chopped garlic, chopped ginger, chillies, fresh coriander and rind in small bowl; sprinkle mixture over curry.

tips ordinary potato or pumpkin can be used instead of sweet potato

turkish pilaf with chicken, onion and almonds

60g butter
500g chicken strips
1 large brown onion (200g), sliced thinly
4 cloves garlic, crushed
⅓ cup (45g) slivered almonds
1 teaspoon ground allspice
½ teaspoon ground cinnamon
3 drained anchovies, chopped coarsely
2 tablespoons dried currants
1½ cups (300g) basmati rice
2 cups (500ml) chicken stock
1 cup (250ml) water
1 fresh long red chilli, chopped finely

preparation time 15 minutes ▓ cooking time 40 minutes ▓ serves 4

1 Melt a third of the butter in large saucepan; cook chicken, in batches, until just cooked through.
2 Melt remaining butter in same pan; cook onion, garlic and nuts, stirring, until onion softens. Add spices, anchovies and currants; cook, stirring, 2 minutes. Add rice; cook, stirring, 2 minutes. Add stock and the water; bring to a boil. Reduce heat; simmer, covered tightly, 20 minutes or until rice is just tender.
3 Stir chicken into pilaf mixture; cook, covered, until heated through. Serve pilaf sprinkled with chilli, and parsley, if desired.

tips chicken strips can be found in most supermarkets – if unavailable, make them by cutting breasts or thigh fillets into thin strips

beans with spicy sausages

preparation time 20 minutes (plus standing time)
⫷ cooking time 40 minutes ⫷ serves 4

800g spicy beef sausages, chopped
coarsely
1 tablespoon olive oil
1 large white onion (200g), chopped
coarsely
3 cloves garlic, crushed
1 large red pepper (350g), chopped
coarsely
½ teaspoon ground cumin
2 teaspoons sweet smoked paprika
1 teaspoon dried chilli flakes
420g can kidney beans, rinsed, drained
2 x 400g cans crushed tomatoes
2 tablespoons coarsely chopped fresh
oregano

1 Cook sausages, in batches, in large deep saucepan until
browned; drain on absorbent paper.
2 Heat oil in same pan; cook onion, garlic and pepper, stirring,
until onion softens. Add cumin, paprika and chilli; cook, stirring,
about 2 minutes or until fragrant. Add beans and undrained
tomatoes. Bring to a boil then reduce heat; simmer, covered,
20 minutes.
3 Return sausages to pan; simmer, covered, about 10 minutes
or until sausages are cooked through. Remove from heat; stir in
oregano. Serve with flour tortillas, if desired.

⫷ note Dried kidney beans, if used as an alternative, contain a
natural toxin that can cause stomach aches and vomiting, so it
is important to destroy the toxin by preparing the beans properly.
Always soak the dried beans for at least 12 hours. Drain, rinse then
cover the beans with fresh water and boil them vigorously for at
least 10 minutes. The beans should be cooked for around 45 to
60 minutes to make them tender.

fish & seafood

chilli king prawn skewers with pistachio coriander rub

32 uncooked large king prawns (2.2kg)

1 teaspoon ground turmeric

1 teaspoon cumin seeds

1 tablespoon coriander seeds

¼ teaspoon chilli flakes

2 long green chillies, chopped coarsely

2 tablespoons desiccated coconut

2cm piece fresh ginger (10g), grated

2 tablespoons blanched almonds, roasted

2 tablespoons pistachios, roasted

140ml can coconut milk

1 tablespoon vegetable oil

1 tablespoon warm water

2 tablespoons fresh coriander leaves

preparation time 45 minutes ▓ cooking time 10 minutes
▓ serves 4

1 Shell and devein prawns. Thread four prawns onto each bamboo skewer.

2 Blend or process spices, green chilli, coconut, ginger, nuts, coconut milk and oil until mixture forms a paste. Transfer to small bowl; stir in the water.

3 Rub paste into prawns; cook skewers on heated oiled grill plate (or grill or barbecue), brushing occasionally with remaining paste, until prawns are changed in colour and cooked thoroughly.

4 Serve skewers sprinkled with coriander leaves.

tips you need to soak eight bamboo skewers in water for at least an hour before using to prevent them splintering and scorching

Yellow curry paste is fairly mild and, due to the inclusion of turmeric, is the one that most closely resembles an Indian curry in flavour. This fish curry is not unlike some of the curries found on the west coast of India, those from Goa or Kerala, areas from which traders sailed east, taking many of their culinary influences to Thailand.

fish yellow curry

preparation time 20 minutes ▓ cooking time 20 minutes ▓ serves 4

8 baby new potatoes (320g), halved
400ml can coconut milk
¼ cup (70g) yellow curry paste
¼ cup (60ml) fish stock
2 tablespoons fish sauce
1 tablespoon lime juice
1 tablespoon grated palm sugar
800g firm white fish fillets, cut into 3cm pieces
3 spring onions, sliced thinly
⅓ cup coarsely chopped fresh coriander
1 fresh long red chilli, sliced thinly
1 tablespoon finely chopped fresh coriander

1 Boil, steam or microwave potatoes until just tender; drain.
2 Meanwhile, place half of the coconut milk in large saucepan; bring to a boil. Boil, stirring, until milk reduces by half and the oil separates from the coconut milk. Add curry paste; cook, stirring, about 1 minute or until fragrant. Add remaining coconut milk, stock, sauce, juice and sugar; cook, stirring, until sugar dissolves.
3 Add fish and potatoes to pan; cook, covered, about 3 minutes or until fish is cooked. Stir in onion and coarsely chopped coriander.
4 Divide curry among serving bowls; sprinkle with chilli and finely chopped coriander.

grilled snapper with spicy tomato and lime sauce

preparation time 15 minutes ▓ cooking time 15 minutes ▓ serves 4

2 tablespoons olive oil

3 cloves garlic, crushed

3 spring onions (75g), chopped finely

425g can chopped tomatoes

1 teaspoon crushed chilli

2 teaspoons white sugar

1 tablespoon lime juice

4 snapper fillets (800g)

75g baby spinach leaves

1 Heat half the oil in small frying pan; cook garlic and onion, stirring, about 1 minute or until onion softens. Stir in undrained tomatoes, chilli, sugar and half the juice. Bring to a boil then reduce heat; simmer, uncovered, about 10 minutes or until liquid has reduced by half.

2 Meanwhile, cook fish in lightly oiled, heated large frying pan until cooked as desired.

3 Place spinach in medium bowl with combined remaining juice and oil; toss gently to combine. Serve fish with spicy sauce and spinach salad.

slow-cooked spicy garlic prawns

preparation time 20 minutes ▇ cooking time 30 minutes (plus refrigeration time) ▇ serves 8

2kg uncooked medium king prawns
4 cloves garlic, crushed
2 fresh long red chillies, chopped coarsely
¾ cup (180ml) olive oil
½ cup (125ml) lemon juice
1 teaspoon sweet paprika
½ cup loosely packed fresh flat-leaf parsley leaves
½ cup loosely packed fresh coriander leaves
¼ cup coarsely chopped fresh chives

1 Preheat oven to slow (150°C/130°C fan-assisted).
2 Shell and devein prawns, leaving tails intact.
3 Combine garlic, chilli, oil, juice and paprika in shallow 3-litre (12-cup) baking dish. Add prawns; toss gently to coat prawns in mixture. Cook, covered, about 30 minutes or until prawns are just cooked through; stir once halfway through cooking time. Cover; refrigerate 2 hours.
4 Serve prawns tossed with herbs.

chilli-seared tuna with avocado cream, tortillas and grilled corn

preparation time 30 minutes (plus standing and refrigeration times) ▦ cooking time 25 minutes ▦ serves 4

4 chipotle chillies

1 tablespoon olive oil

1 small brown onion (80g), chopped finely

2 cloves garlic, crushed

⅓ cup loosely packed fresh oregano leaves

2 tablespoons tomato paste

2 tablespoons water

4 x 200g tuna steaks

2 trimmed corn cobs (500g)

8 large flour tortillas

2 limes, cut into wedges

avocado cream

2 small avocados (400g), chopped coarsely

½ cup (120g) sour cream

¼ cup coarsely chopped fresh coriander leaves

1 tablespoon lime juice

1 Place chillies in small heatproof bowl of boiling water; stand 15 minutes. Drain; chop chillies coarsely.

2 Heat oil in small frying pan; cook onion and garlic, stirring, until onion softens. Stir in chilli, oregano, paste and the water; bring to a boil. Remove from heat; blend or process, pulsing, until mixture forms thick paste.

3 Place fish, in single layer, in large shallow dish; using fingers, pat chilli paste into both sides of fish. Cover; refrigerate 30 minutes.

4 Meanwhile, make avocado cream.

5 Cook corn on heated oiled grill plate (or grill or barbecue) until browned lightly and just tender; slice thickly, cover to keep warm. Cook undrained fish on same heated oiled grill plate until browned both sides and cooked as desired. Cover; stand 5 minutes. Slice fish thickly.

6 Meanwhile, heat tortillas according to manufacturer's instructions. Divide fish, corn, avocado cream and tortillas among serving plates. Serve with lime wedges.

▦ **avocado cream** Blend or process avocado and sour cream until smooth; stir in coriander and juice.

This curry has its origins in the curries of Penang, an island off the northwest coast of Malaysia, close to the Thai border. The paste is a complex, sweet and milder variation of an authentic Thai red curry paste, which is especially good with seafood.

¼ cup (60g) panang curry paste

¼ cup (60ml) fish sauce

2 tablespoons grated palm sugar

4 fresh kaffir lime leaves, torn

2 tablespoons peanut oil

500g ling fillets, cut into 3cm pieces

500g uncooked medium king prawns

250g scallops

200g green beans, chopped coarsely

½ cup loosely packed fresh thai basil

½ cup (70g) coarsely chopped roasted unsalted peanuts

2 fresh long red chillies, sliced thinly

panang curry paste

(makes 1 cup)

25 dried long red chillies

1 teaspoon ground coriander

2 teaspoons ground cumin

2 cloves garlic, quartered

8 spring onions, chopped coarsely

2 x 10cm sticks (40g) fresh lemon grass, thinly sliced

2cm piece fresh galangal (10g), chopped finely (see glossary)

2 teaspoons shrimp paste

½ cup (75g) roasted unsalted peanuts

2 tablespoons peanut oil

panang fish curry

preparation time 35 minutes ▓ cooking time 35 minutes ▓ serves 4

1 Place coconut milk, paste, sauce, sugar and lime leaves in wok; simmer, stirring, about 15 minutes or until mixture reduces by a third.

2 Meanwhile, heat oil in large frying pan; cook seafood, in batches, until just changed in colour. Drain on absorbent paper.

3 Add beans and seafood to curry mixture; cook, uncovered, stirring occasionally, about 5 minutes or until beans are just tender and seafood is cooked as desired.

4 Serve curry sprinkled with basil, nuts and chilli.

▓ panang curry paste Place chillies in small heatproof jug, cover with boiling water; stand 15 minutes, drain. Meanwhile, dry-fry coriander and cumin in small frying pan over medium heat, stirring until fragrant. Blend or process chillies and spices with remaining ingredients until mixture forms a paste.

tips kaffir lime leaves, available from Asian food stores, are aromatic leaves of a citrus tree and are used similarly to bay leaves or curry leaves ▓ if you have difficulty finding ling fillets, use any white fish fillets instead

dry thai prawn curry

5 dried long red chillies

1.5kg uncooked medium prawns

2 tablespoons coarsely chopped fresh galangal (see glossary)

10cm stick (20g) fresh lemongrass, chopped coarsely

2 tablespoons coarsely chopped coriander root and stem mixture

2 cloves garlic, crushed

1 teaspoon shrimp paste

2 tablespoons vegetable oil

8 fresh kaffir lime leaves, torn

2 tablespoons water

1 tablespoon fish sauce

1 teaspoon caster sugar

1 medium green apple (150g), unpeeled, cut into matchsticks

2 shallots (50g), sliced thinly

½ cup firmly packed fresh coriander leaves

2 fresh long red chillies, sliced thinly

preparation time 10 minutes (plus standing time) ▍ cooking time 15 minutes ▍ serves 4

1 Place dried chillies in small heatproof jug, cover with boiling water; stand 15 minutes, drain.

2 Shell and devein prawns, leaving tails intact.

3 Blend or process soaked chillies, galangal, lemongrass, coriander mixture, garlic, paste, half of the oil and half of the lime leaf until mixture forms a paste.

4 Transfer curry paste mixture to large bowl, add prawns; mix well.

5 Heat remaining oil in wok; stir-fry prawn mixture with remaining lime leaf until prawns are changed in colour. Add the water, sauce and sugar; stir-fry 1 minute. Remove from heat; toss apple, shallot, coriander leaves and fresh chilli into curry.

vegetarian

tomato, olive and radish salad

1½ cups (180g) pitted black
olives
200g baby plum tomatoes
14 medium red radishes (490g),
trimmed, quartered
200g button mushrooms, halved
½ cup fresh flat-leaf parsley
leaves

dressing

2 teaspoons moroccan seasoning
½ teaspoon ground coriander
½ teaspoon sweet paprika
2 tablespoons red wine vinegar
⅓ cup (80ml) extra virgin olive oil

preparation time 15 minutes (plus refrigeration time) ▦ serves 8

1 Combine dressing ingredients in screw-top jar; shake well.
2 Combine salad ingredients in medium bowl with the dressing.
Cover; refrigerate at least two hours before serving.

tips recipe can be prepared a day ahead
– add the dressing up to three hours before
serving ▦ Moroccan seasoning is available
from most Middle-Eastern food stores, spice
shops and major supermarkets

banana chillies with potato and green olive stuffing

40g butter

2 tablespoons olive oil

3 cloves garlic, crushed

2 teaspoons ground cumin

2 teaspoons dried oregano

600g potatoes, diced into 1cm pieces

3 large tomatoes (660g), diced into 1cm pieces

1 cup (120g) pitted green olives, chopped coarsely

2 cups (240g) coarsely grated cheddar cheese

8 red banana chillies (1.3kg)

tomato sauce

1 tablespoon olive oil

1 clove garlic, crushed

1 medium red onion (170g), chopped coarsely

1 tablespoon ground cumin

2 teaspoons dried oregano

2 x 425g cans chopped tomatoes

½ cup (125ml) water

preparation time 50 minutes ▓ cooking time 1 hour 10 minutes ▓ serves 4

1 Preheat oven to moderate (180°C/160°C fan-assisted).

2 Heat butter and oil in large frying pan; cook garlic, cumin, oregano and potato, stirring occasionally, about 10 minutes or until potato browns lightly. Add tomato and olives; cook, stirring, about 10 minutes or until liquid has evaporated. Transfer to large bowl; stir in cheese.

3 Meanwhile, using sharp knife, make small horizontal cut in one chilli 1cm below stem. Make lengthways slit in chilli, starting from horizontal cut and ending 1cm from tip, taking care not to cut all the way through chilli; discard membrane and seeds. Repeat process with remaining chillies. Carefully divide filling among chillies, securing each closed with a toothpick.

4 Make tomato sauce.

5 Place chillies on tomato sauce in dish, cover; cook about 40 minutes or until chillies are tender. Serve chillies with tomato sauce and a mixed green salad, if desired.

▓ tomato sauce Heat oil in large deep flameproof baking dish; cook garlic, onion, cumin and oregano, stirring, until onion softens. Add undrained tomatoes and the water. Bring to a boil then reduce heat; simmer, uncovered, 10 minutes.

chilli-glazed sweet potato

preparation time 10 minutes ▊ cooking time 1 hour ▊ serves 4

1.5kg sweet potatoes, unpeeled
¼ cup (60ml) sweet chilli sauce
1 teaspoon brown mustard seeds
2 tablespoons coarsely chopped
fresh rosemary

1 Preheat oven to hot (220°C/200°C fan-assisted).
2 Halve sweet potatoes lengthways; cut each half into 2cm wedges.
3 Combine remaining ingredients in large bowl, add sweet potatoes; toss sweet potatoes to coat in mixture. Divide sweet potato mixture between two large shallow baking dishes. Roast about 1 hour or until they are tender and slightly caramelised.

spicy roasted pumpkin couscous

preparation time 10 minutes ▦
cooking time 20 minutes ▦ serves 4

1 tablespoon olive oil

2 cloves garlic, crushed

1 large red onion (300g), sliced thickly

500g pumpkin, peeled, chopped coarsely

3 teaspoons ground cumin

2 teaspoons ground coriander

1 cup (200g) couscous

1 cup (250ml) boiling water

20g butter

2 tablespoons coarsely chopped fresh flat-leaf parsley

1 Preheat oven to 220°C/200°C fan-assisted.

2 Heat oil in medium flameproof baking dish; cook garlic, onion and pumpkin, stirring, until lightly browned. Add spices; cook, stirring, about 2 minutes or until fragrant.

3 Roast pumpkin mixture, uncovered, in preheated oven, about 15 minutes or until pumpkin is just tender.

4 Meanwhile, combine couscous with the water and butter in large heatproof bowl; cover, stand about 5 minutes or until liquid is absorbed, fluffing with fork occasionally.

5 Add pumpkin mixture to couscous; stir in parsley.

pumpkin and bean tagine with harissa and almond couscous

20g butter

1 tablespoon olive oil

2 medium brown onions (300g), chopped coarsely

2 cloves garlic, crushed

4cm piece fresh ginger (20g), grated

2 teaspoons ground cumin

2 teaspoons ground coriander

2 teaspoons finely grated lemon rind

1kg pumpkin, chopped coarsely

400g can chopped tomatoes

2 cups (500ml) vegetable stock

400g green beans, cut into 5cm lengths

⅓ cup (55g) sultanas

1 tablespoon honey

¼ cup finely chopped fresh flat-leaf parsley

¼ cup finely chopped fresh mint

harissa and almond couscous

2 cups (500ml) vegetable stock

1 cup (250ml) water

3 cups (600g) couscous

½ cup (70g) roasted slivered almonds

1 tablespoon harissa

preparation time 30 minutes ▓ cooking time 30 minutes ▓ serves 6

1 Heat butter and oil in large saucepan; cook onion and garlic, stirring, 5 minutes. Add ginger, spices and rind; cook about 1 minute or until fragrant.
Add pumpkin, undrained tomatoes and stock; bring to a boil. Simmer, covered, about 15 minutes or until pumpkin is just tender.
2 Meanwhile, make harissa and almond couscous.
3 Add beans to tagine mixture; cook, stirring, 5 minutes. Stir sultanas, honey and chopped herbs through tagine off the heat just before serving with couscous.

▓ harissa and almond couscous Bring stock and the water to a boil in medium saucepan; remove from heat. Add couscous; cover, stand about 5 minutes or until liquid is absorbed, fluffing with fork occasionally. Gently mix nuts and harissa through couscous.

Tamarind is the product of a native tropical African tree that grows as high as 25 metres. The tree produces clusters of brown 'hairy' pods, each filled with seeds and a viscous pulp that are dried and pressed into the blocks of tamarind found in supermarkets and Asian food stores.

potato and cheese kofta with tomato tamarind sauce

preparation time 30 minutes ▓ cooking time 35 minutes (plus standing time) ▓ serves 4

2 medium potatoes (400g)
2 tablespoons finely chopped fresh coriander
½ cup (75g) roasted unsalted cashews, chopped finely
½ cup (60g) frozen peas, thawed
vegetable oil, for deep-frying
4 hard-boiled eggs, halved

cheese
1 litre (4 cups) milk
2 tablespoons lemon juice

tomato tamarind sauce
1 tablespoon olive oil
1 clove garlic, crushed
3cm piece fresh ginger (15g), grated
½ teaspoon dried chilli flakes
1 teaspoon ground cumin
1 teaspoon ground coriander
½ teaspoon mustard seeds
¼ cup (85g) tamarind concentrate
2 x 400g cans crushed tomatoes

1 Make cheese. Make tomato tamarind sauce.
2 Meanwhile, boil, steam or microwave potato until tender; drain. Mash potato in large bowl; stir in cheese, coriander, nuts and peas.
3 Heat oil in wok; deep-fry level tablespoons of the potato (kofta) mixture, in batches, until cooked through. Drain on absorbent paper.
4 Add koftas to tomato tamarind sauce; simmer, uncovered, 5 minutes. Divide koftas and sauce among serving plates; top with egg.

▓ cheese Bring milk to a boil in medium saucepan; remove from heat, stir in juice. Cool 10 minutes. Pour through muslin-lined sieve into medium bowl; stand cheese mixture in sieve over bowl 40 minutes. Discard liquid in bowl.

▓ tomato tamarind sauce Heat oil in large saucepan; cook garlic and ginger, stirring, until fragrant. Add chilli, spices and seeds; cook, stirring, 1 minute. Add tamarind and undrained tomatoes; bring to a boil. Simmer, uncovered, 5 minutes.

chickpeas in spicy tomato sauce

2 tablespoons ghee

2 teaspoons cumin seeds

2 medium brown onions (300g), chopped finely

2 cloves garlic, crushed

4cm piece fresh ginger (20g), grated

1 tablespoon ground coriander

1 teaspoon ground turmeric

1 teaspoon cayenne pepper

2 tablespoons tomato paste

2 x 400g cans chopped tomatoes

2 cups (500ml) water

2 x 420g cans chickpeas, rinsed, drained

1 large sweet potato (500g), cut into 1.5cm pieces

300g spinach, trimmed, chopped coarsely

preparation time 15 minutes ▓ cooking time 45 minutes ▓ serves 6

1 Heat ghee in large saucepan; cook seeds, stirring, until fragrant. Add onion, garlic and ginger; cook, stirring, until onion softens. Add spices; cook, stirring, until fragrant. Add tomato paste; cook, stirring, 2 minutes.

2 Add undrained tomatoes, the water, chickpeas and sweet potato; simmer, covered, stirring occasionally, for about 30 minutes or until sweet potato is tender and mixture thickens slightly.

3 Stir in spinach just before serving.

This recipe gets its heat from the cayenne, the ground dried pods of a special variety of pungent chilli. Vegetarians will be delighted with the chickpeas as a main course served with raita, and Indian breads such as chapati, poori or paratha.

The word dhal is the Hindi word for legumes and pulses. Regarded as meat substitutes, they feature widely in Indian cooking because they are a good source of protein for this largely vegetarian nation.

mixed dhal

2 tablespoons ghee

1 medium brown onion (150g), chopped finely

2 cloves garlic, crushed

4cm piece fresh ginger (20g), grated

1½ tablespoons black mustard seeds

1 long green chilli, chopped finely

1 tablespoon ground cumin

1 tablespoon ground coriander

2 teaspoons ground turmeric

½ cup (100g) brown lentils

⅓ cup (65g) red lentils

⅓ cup (85g) yellow split peas

⅓ cup (85g) green split peas

400g can crushed tomatoes

2 cups (500ml) vegetable stock

1½ cups (375ml) water

140ml can coconut cream

preparation time 15 minutes ▥ cooking time 1 hour 10 minutes ▥ serves 4

1 Heat ghee in large saucepan; cook onion, garlic and ginger, stirring, until onion softens. Add seeds, chilli and spices; cook, stirring, until fragrant.

2 Add lentils and peas to pan. Stir in undrained tomatoes, stock and the water; simmer, covered, stirring occasionally, about 1 hour or until lentils are tender.

3 Just before serving, add coconut cream; stir over low heat until heated through.

okra and tomato in coconut sauce

preparation time 15 minutes
▥ cooking time 30 minutes
▥ serves 4

5 cloves garlic, quartered
3 shallots (75g), chopped coarsely
2 fresh long red chillies, chopped coarsely
2 spring onions, chopped finely
⅓ cup (100g) tamarind concentrate
1 tablespoon vegetable oil
400g can coconut milk
2 tablespoons lime juice
10 fresh curry leaves
500g fresh okra, halved lengthways
400g can crushed tomatoes

1 Blend or process garlic, shallots, chilli, onions and tamarind until smooth.
2 Heat oil in large saucepan; add tamarind mixture. Cook, stirring, 2 minutes. Add coconut milk, juice and curry leaves; simmer, uncovered 5 minutes.
3 Add okra and undrained tomatoes; simmer, uncovered, about 20 minutes or until okra is tender.

Okra, also known as bamia, bhindi or ladies fingers, is an African vegetable transported all over the world by African slaves and traders. Okra resembles a large green chilli with outer ribs and edible, gummy seeds inside. It can be stewed, as here, roasted or deep-fried, and is as good eaten on its own as it is used in stews, casseroles and soups.

This luscious spinach and cheese dish comes from northern India, the home of paneer, a fresh cow's milk cheese similar to ricotta. It's sold near the fetta and haloumi in supermarkets; either of these two cheeses can replace paneer here, but the results won't be exactly the same.

palak paneer

1 tablespoon vegetable oil
1 teaspoon cumin seeds
1 teaspoon fenugreek seeds
2 teaspoons garam masala (see page 50)
1 large brown onion (200g), chopped finely
1 clove garlic, crushed
1 tablespoon lemon juice
500g spinach, trimmed, chopped coarsely
¾ cup (180ml) cream
2 x 100g packets paneer cheese, cut into 2cm pieces

preparation time 10 minutes ▓ cooking time 20 minutes
▓ serves 6

1 Heat oil in large frying pan; cook spices, onion and garlic, stirring, until onion softens.
2 Add juice and half of the spinach; cook, stirring, until spinach wilts. Add remaining spinach; cook, stirring, until wilted.
3 Blend or process spinach mixture until smooth; return to pan; stir in cream. Add paneer; cook over low heat, uncovered, stirring occasionally, about 5 minutes or until heated through.

Cauliflower is a popular choice for vegetarian curries because it's both filling and, while it has a great taste of its own, the texture of the florets captures the sauce.

cauliflower and green pea curry

preparation time 20 minutes ▦ cooking time 30 minutes
▦ serves 4

600g cauliflower florets
2 tablespoons ghee
1 medium brown onion (150g), chopped finely
2 cloves garlic, crushed
2cm piece fresh ginger (10g), grated
¼ cup (75g) hot curry paste
¾ cup (180ml) single cream
2 large tomatoes (440g), chopped coarsely
1 cup (120g) frozen peas
1 cup (280g) plain yogurt
3 hard-boiled eggs, sliced thinly
¼ cup finely chopped fresh coriander

1 Boil, steam or microwave cauliflower until just tender; drain.
2 Meanwhile, heat ghee in large saucepan; cook onion, garlic and ginger, stirring, until onion softens. Add paste; cook, stirring, until mixture is fragrant.
3 Add cream; bring to a boil then reduce heat. Add cauliflower and tomato; simmer, uncovered, 5 minutes, stirring occasionally.
4 Add peas and yogurt; stir over low heat about 5 minutes or until peas are just cooked. Serve curry sprinkled with egg and coriander.

tips we used vindaloo paste in this recipe, but any hot curry paste (red curry paste, for example) would work just as well

drinks

spiced lemon tea

1 litre (4 cups) water

4 tea bags

1 cinnamon stick

2 cardamom pods

4 whole cloves

1 cup (220g) caster sugar

1½ cups (375ml) cold water,
extra

½ cup (125ml) fresh lemon juice

2 cups (500ml) fresh orange juice

1 medium lemon (140g), sliced
thinly

¼ cup coarsely chopped fresh
mint

1 litre (4 cups) mineral water

ice cubes

preparation time 5 minutes ▨ cooking time 5 minutes
(plus refrigeration time) ▨ makes 3 litres (12 cups)

1 Bring the water to a boil in large saucepan; add tea bags,
spices and sugar. Stir over low heat about
3 minutes or until sugar is dissolved; discard tea bags.
Refrigerate until cold.
2 Discard spices then stir in the extra water, juices, lemon and
mint. Just before serving, add mineral water and ice cubes.

▨ **sugar syrup** Stir 1 cup (220g) caster sugar with
1 cup (250ml) water in small saucepan, over low heat, until
sugar dissolves. Bring to a boil then reduce heat; simmer,
uncovered, without stirring, 5 minutes. Remove from heat;
cool to room temperature. Sugar syrup can be stored in
refrigerator for up to three weeks.

classic margarita

preparation time 5 minutes ▓ serves 1

45ml dark tequila
30ml Cointreau
30ml lime juice
30ml sugar syrup (see page 108)
1 cup ice cubes
1 lime, sliced
salt

1 Combine tequila, cointreau, juice, syrup and ice in cocktail shaker; shake vigorously. Rub lime slice around rim of 150ml margarita glass; turn glass upside-down and dip wet rim into saucer of salt. Strain margarita into salt-rimmed glass.
2 Garnish with lime slice.

chilli margarita

preparation time 5 minutes ▓ serves 1

20ml dark tequila
10ml Cointreau
30ml sugar syrup (see page 108)
10ml lime juice
1 red thai chilli, chopped finely
dash Tabasco sauce
1 cup ice cubes

1 Combine ingredients in cocktail shaker; shake vigorously. Strain into 150ml margarita glass.
2 Garnish with a slice of lime and fresh red chilli, if desired.

sangria mexicana

preparation time 15 minutes ▥ serves 4

750ml bottle dry red wine
30ml Cointreau
30ml Bacardi
30ml brandy
½ cup (110g) white sugar
2 cinnamon sticks
½ medium orange, peeled, chopped coarsely
1 medium lime, peeled, chopped coarsely
6 medium strawberries, chopped coarsely
1 cup ice cubes

1 Place ingredients in large jug; stir until well
combined; pour into highball glasses.

lime and
mint cooler

preparation time 10 minutes (plus refrigeration
time) ▥ cooking time 5 minutes ▥ serves 4

1 cup (250ml) lime juice
1.25 litres (5 cups) chilled mineral water
¼ cup coarsely chopped fresh mint
½ quantity sugar syrup (see page 108)

1 Make sugar syrup.
2 Combine syrup in large jug with juice, mineral
water and mint. Serve immediately, with ice if
desired.

moroccan mint tea

preparation time 10 minutes (plus refrigeration time) ▊ makes 1 litre (4 cups)

1 litre (4 cups) hot water
3 tea bags
1 cup loosely packed fresh mint leaves
2 tablespoons caster sugar
½ cup loosely packed fresh mint leaves, extra
1 cup ice cubes

1 Combine the water, tea bags, mint and sugar in medium heatproof jug, stand 10 minutes; discard tea bags. Cover; refrigerate until cool.
2 Strain tea mixture; discard leaves. Stir in extra mint and ice cubes; serve immediately.

glossary

allspice or jamaican pepper or pimento; so-named because it tastes like a combination of nutmeg, cumin, clove and cinnamon. Available whole (a dark-brown berry the size of a pea) or ground, and used in both sweet and savoury dishes.

almonds flat, pointed nuts having a pitted brown shell enclosing a creamy white kernel that is covered by a brown skin.

blanched brown skins removed.

slivered small pieces cut lengthways.

aubergine also known as brinjal or eggplant; ranges in size from tiny to very large and in colour from pale green to deep purple.

pea also known as makeua puong, slightly larger than a green pea and of similar shape and colour; sold fresh, in bunches like grapes, or pickled packed in jars. Available in Asian grocery stores.

bay leaf aromatic leaves from the bay tree used to flavour soups, stocks and casseroles.

beans

black an earthy-flavoured dried bean; also known as turtle beans or black kidney beans.

green also known as french or string beans (although the tough string they once had has generally been bred out of them), this long thin fresh bean is consumed in its entirety once cooked.

kidney medium-size red bean, slightly floury in texture yet sweet in flavour; sold dried or canned, it is found in bean mixes and in chile con carne (see page 31).

sprouts also known as bean shoots; tender new growths of assorted beans and seeds germinated for consumption.

burrito a dish comprised of wheat flour tortillas wrapped to encase shredded meat, beans and cheese. The ends are turned in to contain the filling.

capers the grey-green buds of a warm climate shrub, sold either dried and salted or pickled in a vinegar brine; tiny young capers, called baby capers, are available both in brine or dried in salt. Must be rinsed well before using.

caraway seeds small, half-moon-shaped dried seeds from a member of the parsley family; adds a sharp anise flavour to both sweet and savoury dishes.

cardamom one of the world's most expensive spices; has a distinctive aromatic, sweetly rich flavour. Purchase in pod, seed or ground form.

cashews plump, kidney-shaped, golden-brown nuts having a distinctive sweet, buttery flavour; they have a high fat content, so should be kept, sealed tightly, under refrigeration to avoid becoming rancid. We use roasted unsalted cashews in this book, available from most supermarkets.

chickpeas also called channa, garbanzos or hummus; a sandy-coloured, irregularly round, legume, often used in Hispanic and Mediterranean cooking. Firm texture, even after cooking, and a floury consistency with a robust, nutty flavour; available canned or dried (the latter need several hours reconstituting in cold water).

chilli available in many types and sizes. Use rubber gloves when seeding and chopping fresh chillies as they can burn your skin. Removing seeds and membranes lessens the heat level.

cayenne pepper a thin-fleshed, long, extremely hot, dried red chilli, usually purchased ground; both arbol and guajillo chillies are the fresh sources for cayenne.

chipotle chillies also known as ahumado chillies, they are dried, smoked jalapeños. They have a deeply intense smoky flavour rather than a blast of heat. They average 6cm in length and are dark brown, almost black.

flakes, dried deep-red very fine dried slices and whole seeds; good for cooking or for sprinkling over cooked food.

green any unripened chilli; also some particular varieties that are ripe when green, such as jalapeño, habanero, poblano or serrano.

jalapeños pronounced hah-lah-pain-yo. Fairly hot, green chillies, available bottled in brine or fresh from greengrocers.

powder the Asian variety, made from dried ground thai chillies, is the hottest; it can be used as a substitute for fresh chillies in the proportion of ½ teaspoon ground chilli powder to 1 medium chopped fresh chilli.

thai red small, medium hot, and bright red in colour.

chorizo Spanish sausage made of coarsely ground pork and highly seasoned with garlic and chilli.

cinnamon stick dried inner bark of the shoots of the cinnamon tree; the stick, once ground, is what we use as cinnamon powder.

cloves dried flower buds of a tropical tree; can be used whole or in ground form. They have a strong scent and taste so should be used sparingly.

coconut

cream in cans and cartons; made from coconut and water.

milk not the juice inside the fruit, which is known as coconut water, but the diluted liquid that comes from the second pressing of the white meat of a mature coconut. Coconut cream comes from the first pressing.

coriander also known as pak chee, cilantro or chinese parsley; bright-green-leafed herb with a pungent flavour. Stems and roots of coriander are also used in South-East Asian cooking; wash well before chopping. Coriander is also available as seeds and in ground form; these must never be used to replace fresh coriander, or vice versa, as the tastes are completely different.

couscous a fine, grain-like cereal product made from semolina. A semolina flour and water dough is sieved then dehydrated to produce minuscule, even-sized pellets of couscous; it is rehydrated by steaming or with the addition of a warm liquid and swells to three or four times its original size; eaten like rice with a tagine, as a side dish or salad ingredient.

cumin also known as zeera; related to the parsley family. Has a spicy, nutty flavour. Available in seed form or dried and ground.

curry

leaves available fresh and dried; buy fresh leaves at Indian food shops. Used to give extra flavour and depth to curries.

powder a blend of various ground spices, available mild or hot; may include chilli, cumin, cinnamon, coriander, fennel, fenugreek, mace, cardamom and turmeric.

dill also known as dill weed; used fresh or dried, in seed form or ground; has a sweet anise/celery flavour with distinctive feathery, frond-like fresh leaves.

fennel also known as finocchio or anise; a crunchy green vegetable slightly resembling celery; also sometimes the name given to the dried seeds of the plant, which have a stronger licorice flavour.

fenugreek hard, dried seed of the aromatic plant native to Asia and southern Europe; has a pleasantly bitter, yet slightly sweet, taste.

fish sauce called naam pla or nuoc naam. Made from pulverised salted fermented fish; has a pungent smell and strong taste, Use according to your taste.

galangal

fresh also known as ka, a rhizome with a hot ginger-citrusy flavour; used similarly to ginger.

pickled also known as ka dong, is used both in cooking and as a condiment served with various noodle and chicken dishes. It is sold cryovac-packed or in jars in Asian grocery stores.

garam masala a blend of spices originating in North India. Used as a base for a curry paste or on its own sprinkled over dishes (see page 50).

ghee clarified butter with the milk solids removed; this fat can be heated to a high temperature without burning.

ginger

fresh also known as green or root ginger; the thick gnarled root of a tropical plant.

ground also known as powdered ginger; cannot be substituted for fresh ginger.

harissa a North African paste made from dried red chillies, garlic, olive oil and caraway seeds; can be used as a rub for meat, an ingredient in sauces and dressings, or eaten on its own as a condiment. It is available, ready-made, from Middle-Eastern food shops and some supermarkets.

kaffir lime leaves or bai magrood; look like two glossy dark green leaves joined end to end, forming an hourglass shape. Sold fresh, dried or frozen; dried leaves are less potent so double amount if you are substituting for fresh leaves. A strip of fresh lime peel can be substituted for each kaffir lime leaf.

kalonji seeds also known as nigella; are black, teardrop-shaped seeds used to impart a sharp, almost nutty flavour.

kecap asin an astringent, salty, soy-sauce-based ketchup used in Indonesian recipes.

kecap manis called sieu wan in Thai; a dark, thick, sweet soy sauce used in most South-East Asian cuisines. The soy's sweetness is derived from the addition of either molasses or palm sugar when brewed.

lemongrass a tall, clumping, sharp-edged aromatic tropical grass that smells and tastes of lemon, can be found fresh, dried, powdered and frozen in supermarkets and Asian food shops. Its refreshingly light taste is less citric or 'bitey' than lemon, and carries with it a hint of ginger; however, its similarity to lemon means it marries well with chilli, garlic and coriander.

lentils (red, brown, yellow) dried pulses often identified by and named after their colour. French green lentils are green-blue, tiny lentils with a nutty, earthy flavour and a hardy nature that allows them to be rapidly cooked without disintegrating. They are a local cousin to the famous (and expensive) French lentils du puy.

mustard
mustard seeds black, also known as brown mustard seeds, are more pungent than the white variety; used frequently in curries. Yellow, also know as white mustard seeds are ground for mustard powder and for use in prepared mustards.
wholegrain also known as seeded. A French-style coarse-grain mustard made from crushed mustard seeds and dijon-style french mustard.

oil
cooking-oil spray we use a cholesterol-free cooking spray made from canola oil.
olive made from ripened olives. Extra virgin and virgin are the first and second press of the olives and are therefore considered the best; the extra light or light name on other types refers to taste not fat levels.
vegetable oil any of a number of oils sourced from plant rather than animal fats.

okra also known as bamia, bhindi or lady fingers; a green, ridged, oblong pod with a furry skin used to thicken stews.

onions
brown and white are interchangeable. Their pungent flesh adds flavour to many dishes.
purple shallots also known as pink or asian shallots or homm; eaten fresh, deep-fried as a condiment, pounded in curry pastes or tossed into stir-fries.
red also known as spanish, red spanish or bermuda onion; sweet-flavoured, large, purple-red onion.
shallots also called french shallots, golden shallots or eschalots. Small, elongated, brown-skinned members of the onion family.
spring also known as green, scallion or, incorrectly, shallot; an immature onion picked before the bulb has formed, with a long, bright-green edible stalk.

oregano also known as wild marjoram; has a woody stalk with clumps of tiny, dark green leaves that have a pungent, peppery flavour and are used fresh or dried.

palm sugar also known as nam tan pip, jaggery, jawa or gula melaka; made from the sap of the sugar palm tree. Light brown to black in colour; usually sold in rock-hard cakes. Substitute brown sugar, if unavailable.

paneer a simple, delicate fresh cow-milk cheese used as a major source of protein in the Indian diet. Ricotta can be substituted.

paprika ground dried sweet red pepper (capsicum); there are many types available, including sweet, hot, mild and smoked.

pastes many curry pastes are available in supermarkets. Green curry paste is one of the most popular Thai pastes – along with red, massaman, panang and yellow. Curry pastes are generally used as the basis for curry dishes; may also be made at home using fresh ingredients.

green the hottest of the traditional pastes; contains chilli, garlic, onion, lemongrass, spice, salt, galangal.

korma a rich, mild sauce with a delicate coconut flavour and hints of garlic, ginger and coriander.

rogan josh a paste of medium heat made from fresh chillies or paprika, tomato and spices.

tandoori a paste of medium heat consisting of garlic, tamarind, ginger, coriander, chilli and spices.

shrimp also known as kapi, trasi and blanchan; a strong-scented, very firm preserved paste made of salted dried shrimp. Also sold in slabs or flat cakes, which should be chopped or sliced thinly then wrapped in foil and roasted before use.

pistachios green, delicately flavoured nuts inside hard off-white shells. Available salted or unsalted, shelled or unshelled.

polenta also known as cornmeal; a flour-like cereal made of dried corn (maize) sold ground in different textures; also the name of the dish that is made from it.

poussin a small chicken, which is no more than 6 weeks old and weighs a maximum of 500g.

preserved lemon a North African specialty, the lemon is preserved, usually whole, in a mixture of salt and lemon juice or oil. To use, remove and discard pulp, squeeze juice from rind, then rinse rind well before slicing thinly. Available from specialty food shops.

rice

basmati a white, fragrant long-grained rice; the grains fluff up when cooked. It should be washed several times before cooking.

calrose a medium grain, versatile, rice; can substituted for short- or long-grain rices if necessary.

white long-grain white, elongated grains that remain separate when cooked; an extremely popular steaming rice.

saffron stigma of a member of the crocus family, available ground or in strands; imparts a yellow-orange colour to food once infused. The quality can vary greatly; the best is the most expensive spice in the world.

salsa a chunky sauce served as an accompaniment, often based on tomato, chilli, garlic and onion. May be cooked or uncooked, mild or very spicy.

sesame seeds black and white are the most common of these tiny oval seeds.

spatchcock a term used to describe splitting open a small chicken, then flattening and grilling it.

split peas also known as field peas; green or yellow pulse grown especially for drying, split in half along a centre seam.

star anise a dried star-shaped pod whose seeds have an astringent aniseed flavour.

tamarind brown 'hairy' pods from the tamarind tree filled with seeds and a viscous pulp that are dried and pressed into blocks of tamarind. Gives a sweet-sour, slightly astringent taste to food. Found in Asian supermarkets. **tamarind concentrate** (or paste) the commercial distillation of tamarind juice into a condensed, compacted paste. Thick and purplish-black, it is ready to use, with no soaking or straining required; dilute paste with water according to taste.

thai basil has smallish leaves, and sweet licorice/aniseed taste; available in Asian supermarkets and greengrocers.

tortilla thin, round unleavened bread originating in Mexico. Made from either wheat flour or corn. Can be fried to make crisp taco shells, stuffed with beans, sour cream and cheese and baked (enchiladas), torn into strips and fried to make scoops for salsas (tostaditas), or fried and stacked with a filling (tostadas).

turmeric also known as kamin; must be grated or pounded before use. Fresh turmeric can be substituted with the more common dried powder: use 2 teaspoons of ground turmeric plus a teaspoon of sugar for every 20g of fresh turmeric called for in a recipe.

conversion charts

Measures

The cup and spoon measurements used in this book are metric: one measuring cup holds approximately 250ml; one metric tablespoon holds 20ml; one metric teaspoon holds 5ml.

All cup and spoon measurements are level. The most accurate way of measuring dry ingredients is to weigh them. When measuring liquids, use a clear glass or plastic jug with metric markings. We used large eggs with an average weight of 60g.

WARNING This book contains recipes for dishes made with raw or lightly cooked eggs. These should be avoided by vulnerable people such as pregnant and nursing mothers, invalids, the elderly, babies and young children.

Dry measures

metric	imperial
15g	½oz
30g	1oz
60g	2oz
90g	3oz
125g	4oz (¼lb)
155g	5oz
185g	6oz
220g	7oz
250g	8oz (½lb)
280g	9oz
315g	10oz
345g	11oz
375g	12oz (¾lb)
410g	13oz
440g	14oz
470g	15oz
500g	16oz (1lb)
750g	24oz (1½lb)
1kg	32oz (2lb)

Liquid measures

metric	imperial
30ml	1 fl oz
60ml	2 fl oz
100ml	3 fl oz
125ml	4 fl oz
150ml	5 fl oz (¼ pint/1 gill)
190ml	6 fl oz
250ml	8 fl oz
300ml	10 fl oz (½pt)
500ml	16 fl oz
600ml	20 fl oz (1 pint)
1000ml (1 litre)	1¾pints

Length measures

metric	imperial
3mm	⅛in
6mm	¼in
1cm	½in
2cm	¾in
2.5cm	1in
5cm	2in
6cm	2½in
8cm	3in
10cm	4in
13cm	5in
15cm	6in
18cm	7in
20cm	8in
23cm	9in
25cm	10in
28cm	11in
30cm	12in (1ft)

Oven temperatures

These oven temperatures are only a guide for conventional ovens. For fan-assisted ovens, check the manufacturer's manual.

	°C (Celcius)	°F (Fahrenheit)	gas mark
Very low	120	250	½
Low	150	275-300	1-2
Moderately low	170	325	3
Moderate	180	350-375	4-5
Moderately hot	200	400	6
Hot	220	425-450	7-8
Very hot	240	475	9

index

ARE YOU MISSING SOME COOKBOOKS?

The Australian Women's Weekly Cookbooks are available from bookshops, cookshops, supermarkets and other stores all over the world. You can also buy direct from the publisher, using the order form below.

TITLE	RRP	QTY	TITLE	RRP	QTY
100 Fast Fillets	£6.99		Grills	£6.99	
A Taste of Chocolate	£6.99		Indian Cooking Class	£6.99	
After Work Fast	£6.99		Japanese Cooking Class	£6.99	
Beginners Cooking Class	£6.99		Just For One	£6.99	
Beginners Thai	£6.99		Just For Two	£6.99	
Best Food Fast	£6.99		Kids' Birthday Cakes	£6.99	
Breads & Muffins	£6.99		Kids Cooking	£6.99	
Brunches, Lunches & Treats	£6.99		Kids' Cooking Step-by-Step	£6.99	
Cafe Classics	£6.99		Low-carb, Low-fat	£6.99	
Cafe Favourites	£6.99		Low-fat Food for Life	£6.99	
Cakes Bakes & Desserts	£6.99		Low-fat Meals in Minutes	£6.99	
Cakes Biscuits & Slices	£6.99		Main Course Salads	£6.99	
Cakes Cooking Class	£6.99		Mexican	£6.99	
Caribbean Cooking	£6.99		Middle Eastern Cooking Class	£6.99	
Casseroles	£6.99		Mince in Minutes	£6.99	
Casseroles & Slow-Cooked Classics	£6.99		Moroccan & the Foods of North Africa	£6.99	
Cheap Eats	£6.99		Muffins, Scones & Breads	£6.99	
Cheesecakes: baked and chilled	£6.99		New Casseroles	£6.99	
Chicken	£6.99		New Curries	£6.99	
Chicken Meals in Minutes	£6.99		New Finger Food	£6.99	
Chinese and the foods of Thailand, Vietnam, Malaysia & Japan	£6.99		New French Food	£6.99	
			New Salads	£6.99	
Chinese Cooking Class	£6.99		Party Food and Drink	£6.99	
Christmas Cooking	£6.99		Pasta Meals in Minutes	£6.99	
Chocs & Treats	£6.99		Potatoes	£6.99	
Cocktails	£6.99		Quick & Simple Cooking (Apr 08)	£6.99	
Cookies & Biscuits	£6.99		Rice & Risotto	£6.99	
Cooking Class Cake Decorating	£6.99		Sauces Salsas & Dressings	£6.99	
Cupcakes & Fairycakes	£6.99		Sensational Stir-Fries	£6.99	
Detox	£6.99		Simple Healthy Meals	£6.99	
Dinner Lamb	£6.99		Simple Starters Mains & Puds	£6.99	
Easy Comfort Food (May 08)	£6.99		Soup	£6.99	
Easy Curry	£6.99		Stir-fry	£6.99	
Easy Midweek Meals	£6.99		Superfoods for Exam Success	£6.99	
Easy Spanish-Style	£6.99		Tapas Mezze Antipasto & other bites	£6.99	
Food for Fit and Healthy Kids	£6.99		Thai Cooking Class	£6.99	
Foods of the Mediterranean	£6.99		Traditional Italian	£6.99	
Foods That Fight Back	£6.99		Vegetarian Meals in Minutes	£6.99	
Fresh Food Fast	£6.99		Vegie Food	£6.99	
Fresh Food for Babies & Toddlers	£6.99		Wicked Sweet Indulgences	£6.99	
Good Food for Babies & Toddlers	£6.99		Wok Meals in Minutes	£6.99	
Great Kids' Cakes (May 08)	£6.99				
Greek Cooking Class	£6.99		TOTAL COST:	£	

Mr/Mrs/Ms _____

Address _____

_____ Postcode _____

Day time phone _____ Email* (optional) _____

I enclose my cheque/money order for £ _____

or please charge £ _____

to my: ☐ Access ☐ Mastercard ☐ Visa ☐ Diners Club

Card number | | | | | | | | | | | | | | | | | | |

Expiry date _____ 3 digit security code *(found on reverse of card)* _____

Cardholder's name_____ Signature _____

* By including your email address, you consent to receipt of any email regarding this magazine, and other emails which inform you of ACP's other publications, products, services and events, and to promote third party goods and services you may be interested in.

ACP BOOKS

General manager Christine Whiston
Test kitchen food director Pamela Clark
Editorial director Susan Tomnay
Creative director Hieu Chi Nguyen
Director of sales Brian Cearnes
Marketing manager Bridget Cody
Business analyst Rebecca Varela
Operations manager David Scotto
International rights enquiries Laura Bamford
lbamford@acpuk.com

ACP Books are published by ACP Magazines a division of PBL Media Pty Limited
Group publisher, Women's lifestyle
Pat Ingram
Director of sales, Women's lifestyle
Lynette Phillips
Commercial manager, Women's lifestyle
Seymour Cohen
Marketing director, Women's lifestyle
Matthew Dominello
Public relations manager, Women's lifestyle
Hannah Deveraux
Creative director, Events, Women's lifestyle
Luke Bonnano
Research Director, Women's lifestyle
Justin Stone
ACP Magazines, Chief Executive officer
Scott Lorson
PBL Media, Chief Executive officer
Ian Law

Produced by ACP Books, Sydney.
Published by ACP Books, a division of ACP Magazines Ltd, 54 Park St, Sydney; GPO Box 4088, Sydney, NSW 2001.
phone (02) 9282 8618 fax (02) 9267 9438.
acpbooks@acpmagazines.com.au
www.acpbooks.com.au
Printed and bound in China.

Australia Distributed by Network Services, phone +61 2 9282 8777 fax +61 2 9264 3278
networkweb@networkservicescompany.com.au
United Kingdom Distributed by Australian Consolidated Press (UK),
phone (01604) 642 200 fax (01604) 642 300
books@acpuk.com
New Zealand Distributed by Netlink Distribution Company,
phone (9) 366 9966 ask@ndc.co.nz
South Africa Distributed by PSD Promotions,
phone (27 11) 392 6065/6/7
fax (27 11) 392 6079/80
orders@psdprom.co.za
Canada Distributed by Publishers Group Canada
phone (800) 663 5714 fax (800) 565 3770
service@raincoast.com

A catalogue record for this book is available from the British Library.
ISBN 978-1-903777-23-7
© ACP Magazines Ltd 2008
ABN 18 053 273 546